A Ton of Honey:

Managing Your Hives for Maximum Production

70874 AN APIARY, CALIFORNIA

By Grant F.C. Gillard

A Ton of Honey:
Managing Your Hives for
Maximum Production

By Grant F.C. Gillard

copyright 2012 Grant F.C. Gillard

For more information:

Grant F.C. Gillard
3721 North High Street
Jackson, MO 63755
gillard5@charter.net

Grant F.C. Gillard is a Presbyterian Pastor and Beekeeper. He has been keeping bees since 1981. He speaks at bee conferences and conventions across the nation. Contact him at gillard5@charter.net to check his availability for your next event.

You can find more information about the author at the conclusion of this book, or www.grantgillard.weebly.com

Dedication:

This book is dedicated to Robert Sears, President of the Eastern Missouri Beekeeping Association.

www.easternmobeekeepers.com

Bob has been a friend and a colleague, graciously including me in a number of EMBA events and providing opportunities for me to share a number of my experiences in a variety of venues.

Bob effuses a contagious passion, kindling an apicultural fervor unlike anyone I've ever met. He exhibits a high standard of excellence, topped only by a particular compassion for the beginning beekeeper to insure they get started on the right foot.

He is, truly, a very unique individual, an accomplished beekeeper and I'm blessed to include him in my circle of friends.

A Ton of Honey:
Managing Your Hives for Maximum Production

Table of Contents:

Forward! or Foreword (?)

Every author who has a book to publish is supposed to garner the support of a well-known celebrity to write "the foreword." I like to think of it as the "forward!" like, "let's get going, troops!"

What's a foreword, or in reality, the *fore word*? A foreword is nothing more than the *word* that comes *before*. It's a statement in the front of a book, usually by someone famous who is not the author, saying something congratulatory about the book, perhaps something appealing and effusive about the author.

Sometimes an author will get someone who is a celebrity in the field, a well-known authority on the subject, to write a foreword introducing the book and saying why it is important and what it adds to our knowledge of the subject. A good foreword is supposed to increase the sales potential of the book.

I know when I'm browsing in the bookstore, as I glance at the cover of the book and below the title it says, "Foreword written by [insert name of famous person]" it's supposed to kindle my interest. It's as if to say, "Wow! If this famous person wrote the foreword, this must be one gosh darn good book."

Well, it doesn't work for me in that way. I've never picked up a prospective book, read the foreword and decided whether or not I'm going to buy the book. I usually skip the foreword, anyway. I want to get on to the meat of the subject. And it doesn't really make much difference to me who writes the foreword, famous or infamous.

But this is my book so I'm going to give you the foreword. Take a minute to read this chapter. A good foreword sets the tone for the book. This book, for me is about my passion for keeping bees. It's about my efforts to explore those management practices that make a positive impact on our hives. It's about my quest to maximize my honey harvest and reward my blood, sweat and tears, not to mention the stings.

Well, okay it's not really blood, sweat and tears, but I do put a lot of time and energy into my beekeeping hobby. And I take my share of stings.

I also want to challenge myself as a beekeeper, for if I didn't, I would never know what is possible. Many beekeepers settle for an average of 20 or 30, perhaps 40 pounds of honey when 100 or even 120 pounds per hive is very reachable...if they only knew what to do...and if they would actually do it.

And if they knew that it only takes a little more effort to go from 50 to 70 pounds, I think they'd be interested. But I'm not ready to settle for 50 to 70 pounds. I want to maximize my honey production.

This manuscript is dedicated to those who refuse to settle for the average honey harvest, those who want more from their bees and from life!

Consider for a moment a battle that will be fought between two opposing armies representing two different nations. In order to minimize the bloodshed, each side selects their best soldier to fight the fight, man to man, hand to hand, each side choosing one solitary soldier representing the whole of the nation that backs him. The ultimate decision rests on which one of the two solitary soldiers will come out on top. As expected, the two armies select their best man to represent them. After all, the entire battle lies in the hands of each respective soldier.

One soldier has been hired to fight the battle and is promised a handsome amount of money. The other side asks for a volunteer who is willing to fight for patriotism and nationalistic pride.

Now which soldier would you bet on? I'm going with the passionate soldier who fights for the love of country. Passion inspires vision, and vision empowers desire, and desire releases and energizes action. Action gets things done! Getting things done is the way to reach your goals. Reaching your goals achieves your dreams.

If we have done anything wrong as beekeepers, it's been settling for too little. Beekeeping is often a "hobby" that we "mess with when we have time." Too often we take the road of least persistence. And I see this problem in my generation when it comes to careers, marriages, retirement and many of the options we choose.

Where is the passion for living?   Where is the motivation to do our best?   What happened to our dreams?

One of my good buddies is a golfing enthusiast. He'll golf every chance he gets—rain or shine, sleet or snow.   He finds reasons to go golfing.   He makes up excuses why he has to go golfing.   He carries his golf clubs in his car all the time (never knowing when the opportunity might present itself).   He never goes on vacation without bringing his clubs along (his children refer to the clubs as his "other family," some of his clubs actually have names).   He plays with passion and the joy of his hobby is written all over his face. Every day he wants to do his best and be his best.

That's the passion I want to possess as I keep bees. I want something that will light a fire under me and stoke my internal flames that cannot be quenched or dampened no matter how rigorous the trials.   It's about putting your heart and soul into something.   For me it's beekeeping, and that's what this book is about. Every day I want to do my best and be my best.

When it comes to beekeeping, I've seen people from all walks of life pick up a hive tool and light up a smoker. I've seen those who entered into the vocation solely because they thought beekeeping would make them a decent amount of money (and I believe it can!). I've also seen those who fall in love with their beekeeping hobbies. They become so absorbed into the realm of the social intricacies of the hive that they lose themselves to the extent that they would pay thousands of dollars just for the privilege of keeping honeybees.

Now that's passion.

What do you think it takes to be successful? George Lucas wrote, *"You have to find something you love enough to be able to take risks, jump over the hurdles and break through the brick walls that are always going to be placed in front of you. If you don't have that kind of feeling for what it is you are doing, you'll stop at the first hurdle."*

I've also seen a lot of people who entered beekeeping because it looked "interesting." But I'm not looking for someone who is merely "interested," I'm looking for someone who is committed, someone who is willing to invest themselves in this project.

It's like when the chicken and the pig went walking down the street and they stopped in front of a diner. The diner advertised their morning breakfast special: bacon and eggs.

The chicken turns to the pig and says, "You know, my people were very interested in the making of that breakfast. They gave their time to lay those eggs."

The pig responds, "Yeah? Well my people were totally invested and committed to making that breakfast happen. They gave their lives for that bacon."

This manuscript on managing your hives for maximum production is not for everyone. Actually, beekeeping is not for everyone. A lot of people attempt to keep bees, but soon give up because it's hard work. And those bees sting! Holy cow! Those stings hurt!

Almost everyone I know who starts keeping bees is under the impression it's not hard work "because the bees do all the work." Then there are those people for whom the challenges appear to be too great and the hurdles too high. They just give up too soon if they start at all. And I have a great encouragement for those who tell me every time they see me at the farmer's market they say, "I'm still thinking about getting into bees, would you help me?"

But someday never comes and despite a good aim, they never pull the trigger. But then, beekeeping isn't for everyone. I've often wondered if I'm really helping someone when I start them down this apicultural road. It costs a lot of money to get started. Have done them a favor?

Yet it's still my hope that those passionate few who are willing to invest themselves and commit the necessary energy will find their respective success. I want to write for those who will stick it out and glean what they need from this book to take them to that proverbial Promised Land of higher returns and maximum production.

A legend tells the story of a farmhand named Roscoe. After a long summer day working in the fields, Roscoe was walking home in the twilight of the setting sun. He was so tired he spent most of the walk home with his eyes half-closed. He was walking along road next to the river, mindlessly dreaming of what he could do if he were rich. As he walked his foot struck a leather pouch someone dropped in the road. It felt like it was filled with a collection of small pebbles.

Absentmindedly he picked up the pouch and poured a few of the pebbles into his hand. He began mindlessly throwing the small pebbles into the water. "When I am a rich man," he said to himself, "I'll have a large house."

And he threw another pebble into the river and vowed to wear tailor-made, expensive clothing once he made his fortune. He threw another one and thought, "My wife and I will have servants and rich food, and many other fine things."

And this went on until just one stone was left. As Roscoe held it in his hand, a ray of light from the setting sun caught it and made it sparkle. He then realized that it was no mere pebble, but was instead a valuable gem. He had been throwing away the real riches in his hand, while he wishfully dreamed of unreal riches in the future.

As beekeepers, it's my hope that we would remember all the riches we have as we tend to our bees, riches right at our fingertips. It's also my hope that we do not overlook these riches because of all the things we don't have—many of which we don't even need in order to live a contented and happy life.

As Charles Dickens once said, *"Reflect upon your present blessings, of which every man has plenty; not on your past misfortunes, of which all men have some."*

And even as some of us in this industry have incurred horrible losses, it's my hope that we would develop the capacity to give thanks for what's left rather than worry about what's lost. We can always rebuild. We befriend resilience.

Peace, contentment and happiness come from within and not from without. They come from changing the things we can change, but also from accepting and learning to live with the things we cannot change—in addition to having the wisdom to know the difference. They come from the attitude of one's heart and mind that accepts this world as it is, which is often not as we would have it, if it were but our choice.

Lastly, I leave with you another story that is played out in a lot of motivational seminars on human development. The speaker looks out over his audience and asks for a show of hands of everyone who wants to be a millionaire. As you would expect, all the hands in the room go up. Then the speaker asks for a show of hands of those who feel they have already attained this level of being a millionaire. All the hands go down. After all, that's the reason why they came to hear this speaker.

The speaker then asks who wants to be successful in their respective field of expertise. All the hands in the room go up. Then the speaker asks for a show of hands of those who feel they are presently successful. All the hands fall to their laps.

The speaker then holds up a crisp, $100 dollar bill. He says, "Who wants a hundred dollars?" All the hands in the room go up. He asks again, "Who wants a hundred dollars?" Several people strain to put their hand higher, some wave their hands with great enthusiasm bordering on becoming apoplectic.

The speaker asks again, and a fourth time, then a fifth time. The audience members are still in their seats, many of them waving frantically. Some of them are saying, "I do, I do!"

The speaker asks again, "Who wants this $100 dollar bill?"

And remarkably, one of the audience members in the front row starts to get up. Then he sits back down. Then he gets up and moves halfway toward the podium. But he's not sure what the speaker means. Is he really giving away a hundred dollar bill? He takes another step, but stops. He's timid and hesitant. What's the catch? He walks tentatively to the speaker at the podium. Sensing this is some kind of practical joke or a stunt that is waiting to backfire, the audience member reaches for the $100 dollar bill, and cautiously takes it out of the speaker's hand. But he remains next to the speaker as if the speaker is going to snatch it right back or change his mind.

The speaker smiles warmly and says, "Well, there you go. Now we can get on with today's topic."

The audience quiets down as if this is some joke. The person who got up and retrieved the $100 dollar bill is stunned, still standing alongside the speaker waiting for some kind of repercussion, some kind or recrimination, some kind of rejection for having the nerve to stand up and take the $100 dollar bill.

The speaker turns to this audience member, smiles and again says, "Really. It's yours to keep. I asked who wanted it and you were the only one to come up and get it. And I promise you, it's yours. Put it in your wallet and you can return to your seat."

The audience is silenced in their disbelief, hoping the speaker brings out another $100 dollar bill. They're ready now. But instead he moves on to the first topic of his presentation.

Later in his talk, he relates the exercise to the subject of his presentation. He goes on to describe how many people will say they want something, but few will actually get up and get it. Many people will tell you what they want, but few are willing to take the risks to obtain it. Many people make plans, but few take the necessary action to achieve those plans.

The mind is willing but the flesh doesn't have the energy to see it through. The imagination can envision a goal but the spirit is too easily discouraged to achieve it. And then there are those who are too timid and fearful to even dream of the possibilities.

This is a manuscript about managing your hives for maximum production. It's also a manuscript about giving yourself permission to shoot for higher goals and bigger honey harvests. I want you to dream big.

And keep this in mind: If dreams were easy, we'd be calling them "naps." Dream big!

This book is also a manuscript about keeping honeybees in general. A lot of people have come to me and said they want to keep bees, but only a few have taken the necessary steps to make it happen. Of those people who have taken the steps to buy the equipment and get some bees, a majority will tell me they want to obtain a financial return on their investment. In some cases, your spouse wants to see a financial return! Mostly, new beekeepers want some kind of a payoff on all their work. They share dreams of selling all this honey their bees are willing to produce. But only a scant handful of these people will actually the do the work it takes to achieve these lofty goals.

And in reality, those goals are not that lofty.

In reality, most people just don't want it enough to make it happen. And beekeeping is hard work that you really have to want it in order to succeed with it.

I remember an interesting quote: "Only those who hunger truly lose weight." You have to hunger for weight loss more than you hunger for food. You have to hunger for maximum production more than the sedentary procrastination that paralyzes your steps to action.

Nolen Brushnell, founder of Atari and the Chuck E. Cheese franchise said, "Everyone who has taken a shower has had an idea. It's the person who gets out of the shower, dries off and does something about it who is the one who makes a difference."

As you start out reading this book, determine in your own mind that you are going to be one of those that make it happen. Will you make a difference in your own life? Will you be willing to take the necessary steps and work diligently to see the plan through?

Remember there are three kinds of people in the world.

--those who make it happen,

--those who watch it happen,

--those who wonder how in the
world it happened without them.

Here's hoping you're that first group. Make it happen.

Grant F.C. Gillard

Jackson, Missouri

December 2012

Introduction

This is my latest manuscript I call, "A Ton of Honey: Managing Your Hives for Maximum Production."

As I've talked to beekeepers around the country, and as I've communicated to other beekeepers via bulletin board sites on the Internet, I conclude the highest ideal and the most common goal for most beekeepers is **honey production**. Almost everyone I talk to hopes their hives make a lot of honey. Their spouse hopes they make a lot of honey, too!

Producing a lot of honey is one of the easiest yardsticks that measure your success. Pounds of honey is the qualifying appraisal against which you compare yourself to your peers. But as we all know, there are many different products of the hive. There are several different ways a hive can produce a financial return. Still, honey production is the first and foremost goal of most beekeepers, including me.

I am interested in maximizing the potential of my beehives. My goal is to work with my bees and help them do what they do best: Produce honey.

Initially, I started out keeping bees with the goal of maximizing my yield per hive. Then, as I grew and expanded, I shifted my goal to that of producing a large, total crop of honey. Even side by side, all hives are different and will gather different amounts of nectar and produce different amounts of honey. Instead of pounds per hive, I was shooting for the maximum total production from all my hives put together. The easiest way to maximize my total honey production was to add more hives. But then I began to notice how the individual production from each hive began to slip a little as I added more hives.

Then it dawned on me: to get the maximum total production, I still need to help each hive attain its individual potential. I find myself coming back around to working with each hive, paying attention to the age of the queen, winter feed stores, mite loads, the health of the hive, swarming prevention, and on the list goes. There are many managerial decisions that must be made in order to assist your hives to make that ton of honey.

If you are interested in producing a ton of honey, there are two ways to do it. The first, which is what this book is about, is to work with each hive and help it overcome the challenges that hold it back, then give it the resources it needs to do what it does best, namely, produce honey. This method will take work.

However, if you still want to maximize your total honey crop, you can simply continue to add more and more hives. More hives will produce more honey. But if you've invested time and energy (and lots of money) into these beehives, why not try and bring in the maximum return on your investment? Why not help each hive achieve its potential?

That's where I'm coming from as I sit down to write this book. My goal is to maximize my honey production from each hive.

One of the most common questions I'm asked at bee meetings and conventions is this: how do I get my bees to produce more honey? The biggest element of shame comes from those people who are chagrined as they explain, "Well, I didn't get any honey from my bees this year..."

Then I ask, "Why not?" or "How come?"

And they look at the floor, slowly and reply, "Not really sure. They didn't make any honey last year, either."

The goal of maximizing one's honey production is more common than people are willing to admit. And if you're going to put in the time and energy keeping bees, why not shoot for harvesting the most honey from each hive? What reward could be sweeter?

Along the way to reaching for my goals, I also found there is no one simple answer or single factor to getting the most honey out of your hives. It takes the proper integration of time (and timing) and the physical resources to get the bees to work at their best.

As the beekeeper, it's up to you to help them by giving them the resources they need, when they need them. And when you stop and think about it, our bees are captive to our management. They can only work with the resources we provide. And if we don't provide, well then they can't produce to their potential. On their own, the bees will do alright, even survive without us, but there will be no extra honey for us. It's fascinating how the bees respond to our management.

And it's not enough to just do the right thing; you have to do the right thing at the right time in the right way. Even doing the right thing at the wrong time may be worse than doing nothing at all. And basically, I'm trying to do the right things at the right time to get the most honey from each of my hives.

And that's what this manuscript is all about: getting the most honey from your hives and helping each hive produce up to its potential. Every hive has an untapped potential of productivity.

Beekeepers Have Potential too:

Different people keep bees for different reasons and different purposes. Some beekeepers raise bees to sell nucs or produce queens. Some beekeepers are in the pollination business. Some people just want a few beehives in the back yard so they can watch the bees work or pollinate the garden. That's all good. But this manuscript is about maximizing the production of honey.

And this kind of perspective of maximizing your honey yields is not for everyone. It also depends on your purpose for keeping bees. I keep bees to produce honey, which I then sell to make money. I am a small-scale, part-time commercial beekeeper. Even though I keep bees on a part-time basis (I also have a "regular" day job), I operate as if this were a profit-making business (and many years it is very, very profitable). Beekeeping is a means to bring in extra money, though I'm more apt to plow my profits back into the business though lately my bees have been providing a lot of funding for college tuition.

And understand this fact: I write this manuscript with the assumption and presumption that you want to get your bees to produce a lot of honey. But here's a warning: lots of honey means lots of extraction. It means lots of work. It takes proactive planning. Procrastination will be your downfall. My father-in-law is fond of saying, "Nothing important merely happens." Beekeeping is a lot of work and nothing "merely happens." The work can be intensive at times, but then the "rewards" are very sweet.

Some of my friends are "sideliners." They keep a few bees, maybe upwards to twenty-five hives. They sell a little honey after the harvest and when it's gone, it's gone. If asked, I'm willing to bet they'd shoot for a higher honey production because they know they could sell more honey. These beekeepers have no problem selling their honey, and if they were willing to admit it, they'd like their hives to produce more honey.

Some of my friends are "hobbyists." They keep bees just to have them around and if they get a little honey to give away or sell, that's fine. If they don't, well that's fine too. Mostly, they are just happy to have their bees live through the winter. But if asked, I'll bet they are willing to admit they'd like to get more honey from their hives. Some of these beekeepers would like to have more locations and more hives, but often they are limited by the space of their backyard.

I hope I, in no way, seem to disparage anyone's goals of keeping bees. We all keep bees for different purposes. My purpose is to make lots of honey and invest the resources that make it possible. Obviously, your reasons will differ.

Everyone has a purpose in keeping bees and I think one of the keys to successfully keeping bees is identifying and articulating your purpose. In a nutshell, why do you keep bees? I keep bees as a business, and it is a very enjoyable business. I also seek to make some money at it. My income is derived from honey sales and money is my bottom line.

Interestingly, all three of these categories of commercial, sideliner and hobbyist all seek to get the most honey out of their hives. This goal is not something relegated to the "big boys." And no one needs to feel sheepish admitting they'd like to increase the size of their honey crop.

But this manuscript is not for everyone. A ton of honey takes a lot of work to produce, including a lot of attention to the details, a lot of commitment to working when it's hot and humid, and you have to tolerate getting stung. And after you harvest the honey, every drop of this honey must be extracted and marketed. It's not easy, but for those who are willing to work at it, it doesn't take that much work to be successful.

And let me also add that I enjoy working my bees. It's not really even work! There's an old saying that says, "Those who enjoy what they do never have to go to work." Beekeeping is a labor of love for me. It takes a lot of work, but it's not really even work. I don't really see it as a job.

Producing a ton of honey is not a job for everyone, and that's okay. But if you want to maximize your hive's resources and increase the financial gain for yourself, then sit back and enjoy the ride. After keeping bees since 1981, experiencing a lot of ups and downs, joys and frustration, I'll show you exactly how to get it done.

I also would be remiss if I didn't mention my other resources for beekeepers. Go to my personal web site, www.grantgillard.weebly.com and find the tab that says, "My Books." You'll find the most current list of links that will lead you to find a way to read a sample chapter and another link to order.

Beekeeping With Twenty-five Hives

(Coming soon - check www.grantgillard.weebly.com, "My Books)

This manuscript details my initial entry into beekeeping and how I expanded, turning my hobby into a profitable, income-producing enterprise.

****

Beekeeping 101: Where Can I Keep My Bees?

https://www.createspace.com/4044187

Free Bees:

Finding and Retrieving Feral Swarms

Despite the mites and CCD, there are still quite a few colonies of feral honeybees out there, and each spring they'll swarm. This resource will share secrets of catching and retrieving those swarms that you can incorporate into your beekeeping hobby. Hey! Those bees are out there and they're free!

https://www.createspace.com/4107714

Keeping Honey Bees and Swarm Trapping:

Utilizing Pheromone-Baited Swarm Traps

This is an advanced resource for beekeepers who want to take their swarm catching to the next level. This resource will share with you how to construct bait hives, load them with pheromone lures, and catch all those swarms that no one knows about.

https://www.createspace.com/4106626

Why I Keep Honeybees

(and why you should, too!):

Keys to Your Success

https://www.createspace.com/4043781

****

Check my web site for more additions:

http://www.grantgillard.weebly.com

Chapter 1: Maximizing Potential

Making the Best Use of What You Already Have

Two good ol' boys from southeast Missouri decided they'd go out fishing one day. They hit the lake in their bass boat and the fish were biting like crazy. The first fisherman was pulling in nice big bass and quickly slid them into his cooler of ice. He turned to notice the second fisherman tossing back the big ones and keeping the tiny, six-inch fish.

Perplexed at this paradox, the first fisherman asked, "What are doing throwing those big fish back and keeping the little ones?"

The second fisherman simply shrugged apologetically and said, "Well, my wife only has a small frying pan."

Ridiculous? Absolutely! All he has to do is buy his wife a bigger frying pan. And yet that's how people view their lives. They are too short-sighted to see the big picture and too dim to see the potential solutions. Limited by their beliefs, all they keep are small fish.

Beekeepers are like that, too. But instead of a larger frying pan, I think we need a larger vision of what's possible. Have we really pushed the envelope and started thinking "outside the hive?" Think for just a minute of what we are missing by limiting our vision. I've heard some beekeepers lament, "I don't know what I'm going to do with all that honey. I ought to just leave it for the bees."

And these are the guys with two hives.

Every colony has potential, but not every colony of honeybees is capable of capturing that potential. For instance, let's presume a certain colony of honeybees has the potential for producing 150 - 200 pounds of surplus honey. Will it make that amount? Can it make that amount? Probably not! There are so many other variables that rob the colony of their ability to capture this potential.

As an example: If the queen is young but they don't have enough room to store the nectar they'll swarm and the potential will be cut down. The colony may have all the room needed to store all that nectar, but if the queen is old she won't lay as many eggs as her younger counterpart. Fewer eggs results in a diminished work force to forage blooms. Her lack of productivity inhibits the colony's potential. What if you have a young queen, ample room for egg-laying, but the hive is oppressed by an aggressive infestation of mites or small hive beetles? Yep, a reduction in the honey production.

Now here's the million dollar question: who is responsible for removing these obstacles? Who is responsible for making sure there is ample room to store the incoming nectar? Who is responsible for making sure the queen is young and productive? Who is responsible for mite control? Yep, the beekeeper.

Every colony has a great potential to produce monster honey crops. There are, unfortunately, many factors that have to be met before this rather mythical potential can be realized. Some of these factors are limitations that must be removed; some of these factors are additions that benefit the bees and enhance production. There are also some factors which are merely the implementation of the beekeeper's management, timing and skill. We have to remember that we, as beekeepers, are in charge of this colony. We are stewards. The bees can only perform with the resources we provide, and we have to note how our ignorance can greatly limit their potential.

Beekeepers help create the best environment to capture the honeybees' highest potential of what they are capable of doing. But what a colony is capable of doing is the sum of many factors. Not every colony has the same potential. Not every beekeeper knows to make the right decisions, at the right time, to meet the colony's needs to meet that potential.

It's hard, but not impossible to capture the highest potential of each hive. This is a manuscript to help you assist each colony to reach their potential, but I'm not a miracle worker. Some hives just won't have all the right components to make a ton of honey. And if you're a lazy beekeeper or a habitual procrastinator, then most of my suggestions will be lost. I've met some beekeepers who were so lazy (and frustrated with their lack of honey) that I suggested they switch hobbies to stamp collecting. It's a whole lot easier, though the potential paper cut always looms on the horizon.

It's funny how honeybees can easily survive on their own. Millions of hives are surviving in hollow trees out in the woods and no one bothers them. They produce what they need and they do just fine.

But when we move bees into hive bodies with the intent of harvesting surplus honey, they are at our mercy. We need to remember that not all beehives are alike, no two beekeepers are alike, no two bee yards are alike, and no two seasons are alike. But every managed bee hive has a greater potential than what the bees are doing, and a much, much larger potential than if we just left them alone.

And you'd be surprised at the number of beekeepers I've met that practice the "let alone" method of keeping bees. Basically, they leave the bees alone. They never open the hive. They never requeen. They never do anything to combat the mites. These beekeepers fear anything they do will only cause problems for the bees. Their fear of messing something up causes a "paralysis of analysis." They continue to "think about" doing something rather than actually doing it.

All I can think about is what a waste of time and resources. But if these beekeepers are happy, then I'm wrong to criticize them. Yet as I continue to talk to these beekeepers, it isn't long before they start complaining how they'd like to get some honey one of these years. Sadly, neither these beekeepers nor their hives are working up to their potential.

Every hive has potential, but not all hives have the same potential. It's a lot like those full-page advertisements on the back of old comic books I read when I was a kid. The skinny kid and his girl friend are on the beach. The well-muscled bully kicks sand on the skinny kid, but the poor skinny kid can't do anything to defend himself. So damaged is his self-image, that even the girl friend leaves him for the bully.

So the skinny kid goes home and kicks the television set in his frustration. Then, picking up a comic book like the one I was reading, he reads the same advertisement and sends off for this body building course and the miraculous muscle development equipment. When these items arrive, he works out and exercises to build muscle. He becomes increasingly stronger (all in just ten minutes a day over the course of six weeks, as the advertisement will tell you).

Then the formerly skinny kid returns to the same beach where the bully stole his girl friend. He's now muscular and full of confidence. He confronts the old bully, who still has the former girl friend on his arm, and the formerly skinny kid effortlessly beats up the bully, who in turn, runs away with his proverbial tail between his legs. Then the formerly skinny kid with the new-found confidence wins back his old girl friend and they live happily ever after.

Life is good when you read the back page of comic books. But let's take a closer look at reality.

The advertisement leads the reader to believe that anyone can send off for this body building course and beat up the beach bullies and win back the hearts of their fickle girl friends. (Personally, any woman that superficially fickle isn't worth my time. Yeah, call me bitter.)

Medical science, on the other hand, has proven this kind of muscle growth is not normally the case. There are some body types that simply cannot, and will not, respond this way to physical exercise. The body types described as endomorphs (fat and soft) and ectomorphs (very thin and lean) simply cannot make it happen because they lack the physical potential found in mesomorphs (muscular).

However, everyone, irrespective of their body type, can benefit from a planned program of physical exercise. Maybe not to beat up the bullies on the beach, but at least you'll develop the strength to open a brand-new jar of pickles at your mother-in-law's house. And believe me, opening that jar of pickles is mighty impressive to an old person!

Everyone has potential, but not everyone will become super muscular and beat up bullies on the beach. Everyone has potential, and exercise will help you reach upward toward your highest potential. And while everyone will not turn into a muscular body type, the point is exercise will help you improve what you already have. You are better off with exercise than without it.

The same is true for honeybees. Every colony has potential. However, not every hive will give you 150 – 200 pounds of surplus honey. Not every hive has this high level of potential, not every hive exists in an environment with enough forage to support this level of production, but every hive still has a potential that responds to prudent and proactive management.

For example, some hives have a genetically determined slow rate of build up in the spring. They may only have the potential for 80 pounds of surplus honey. Perhaps you have an area that lacks certain seasonal, floral sources that limits their potential even with great genetics for a spring build up. You may have an area that just doesn't grow a variety of nectar-producing plants. (It always surprises me how inner city and roof-top hives flourish in the urban environment).

You may have a race of bees that experiences an explosive spring build up. However, many of these colonies also have a greater propensity to swarm. You lose the greater potential because you didn't alleviate the congestion and your procrastination allowed these hives swarm. You may have a hive that superseded the queen with a genetically inferior replacement without your knowledge. You may have a year in which it rains six days out of the week or a drought turns your forage area into a desert.

There are many factors that determine potential and influence the results, yet every colony has untapped potential. Our job as beekeepers is to manage the variable factors and bring our hives into the true potential.

And you have to remember there are things we can change and then there are things we can't change. Wisdom knows the difference, yet prudence will tackle those variables we can change. Sadly, a lot of beekeepers I know just like to complain about the things they can change but they are too lazy to work out those variables.

I believe every hive has the potential to produce beyond their levels of normal, present achievement, a greater potential than if simply left to take "nature's course of action." The difference is management, and management is you. You hold the key to assisting the bees and their abilities, in addition to enhancing the environment to produce more honey.

Sound management will benefit every colony irrespective if the colonies are weak or strong, irrespective of breed of bee or location of floral sources. Sound management develops and fulfills the potential that exists, the potential that would otherwise go unfulfilled if you did nothing but sit around your house and grumble in frustration because your bees aren't producing any surplus honey.

And to those who complain they didn't get any honey last year, I simply have to say, "Hey! What are you doing? What are you not doing?" There sins of omission as well as sins of commission! But the buck stops with you, the beekeeper. Don't blame the mites, do something about them. Don't criticize your queen, replace her. Be a steward. Be responsible. Take action.

I also believe beekeepers have potential to be first-rate, crackerjack beekeepers that produce an average of several hundred pounds per hive. Yet some of us don't have the time to fulfill this potential. We all have family obligations and work commitments.

Some of us don't have all the equipment we need or the money to buy what would make our job as beekeepers easier. Some of us don't have the inclination or the motivation (What would I do with all that honey?) to fulfill the potential. Some of us are just plain lazy and inattentive of our hives. Then there are the procrastinators.

Don't get me started about your lack of success because you procrastinated. And ignorance is no excuse! Join the local bee club. Attend the state meetings. Read a few books. Subscribe to the *American Bee Journal* or the *Bee Culture* and read the darn things when they arrive in the mail. Find a mentor. Get your head out of your....Okay, Grant, settle down. Breathe.

We all have potential, but not every one of us has the same potential. But the point I want to make is that if you read and study, if you observe your bees and pay attention to what they are doing, if you make it a point to join a beekeeper's club to learn more, you will be better off than if you merely put those bees in a box and let them go and do their thing.

Every beekeeper has potential to improve his or her management. Every hive has potential to respond to our management. But not every hive has the same potential. There are many factors, and many interrelated components. But I am firmly convinced that every hive can produce more honey than it already does; every beekeeper can do more than he or she does.

Chapter 2: The Secret is Really

Not a Secret

A better title for this manuscript would be the nefarious, "Secrets to Maximum Honey Production!" But honestly, there are no secrets; only sound management. Yet if I entitled this report, "Things You Are Responsible For In Order To Get The Most Honey," I doubt anyone would turn the first page. That sounds like too much work. I also considered something of an academic nature in, "The Interrelated Components of an Integrated Production Scheme." Nah. Too stuffy.

Management is what brings in the honey, and producing the highest honey yield is where it's at. So I settled for the title of, "A Ton of Honey: Managing Your Hives for Maximum Production." It's basically a manuscript that could be called, "High Yield Honey Production." It tells you the benefits of trying to get your hives to live up to their potential, to produce the maximum amount of honey they are capable of producing.

If maximum honey yields sounds too utilitarian to you, consider what the late Roger Morse wrote in his book, "Rearing Queen Honey Bees." He refers to criticism he received for placing what other people thought was too much emphasis on honey production. In his defense, he noted how some beekeepers keep bees just for fun. He also noted how some people keep bees for their therapeutic value. Though people have different reasons, Morse believes the person who seeks to maximize his or her bees' honey production gets the most in terms of profit and enjoyment whatever their reason for keeping bees might be.

In the spirit of Roger Morse, it's my intention to help you integrate the management techniques which bring high productivity, or in other words, maximizing the hives potential so you can harvest the highest possible honey yields. To call this manual a book of "secrets" brings about an air of romance and tinge of intrigue.

As you read this manuscript, you may conclude, "Wait a minute. There are no secrets and most of this is nothing but common sense."

It is. But not everyone uses common sense. Common sense is most uncommon. Even when it is known, it is seldom practiced. Procrastination, laziness, time conflicts and misdirected motivation all lead to the diminished status of common sense. We just don't do it. We don't do what we should be doing, and we do the things that we shouldn't. We are a contradiction of intent and practice. The spirit is willing but the flesh is weak. Most of us need to be reminded of all the things we need to do. Even then, we're not too anxious to do it, even when we know what has to be done.

I confess that most of my suggestions are nothing more than basic beekeeping principles. There are no secrets. There are no tricks, no magic bullets. But it isn't so much of what you do as it is when and how you do it, and by golly, the fact that you actually remember to do it. This is a manuscript that details the significant relationship between timing, management skills and the execution and implementation of those skills. But you also have to count the significance of the integration of all these factors. Beekeeping is more than the sum of all its parts.

I believe in assisting the bees to produce their greatest potential for producing honey. I also believe in helping the beekeeper get the greatest potential joy and happiness from his or her bees. When you help the bees, I believe you will help yourself.

As you read on, remember to keep your needs and potential for enjoyment in mind as well as the bees' potential to bring in a maximum crop of honey.

Chapter 3: What are You Really Looking For?

Preparing the Beekeeper for Maximum Honey Yields

On their own, bees gather enough honey to meet their needs. Yet there's no question that honeybee colonies have to be prepared, proactively, to gather and store large crops of surplus honey to meet the expectations of the beekeeper. So let's start out by remembering the most important cog in this wheel of honey production: the beekeeper.

You need to be prepared, proactively, just as much as the colonies to produce these record crops of honey. You need to be prepared physically, but also intellectually, mentally and philosophically!

C.C. Miller once said, and I paraphrase, *"Almost every beekeepers dreams of producing the most honey from his hives, then dreads how in the world he is going to get rid of it."*

Really? Do you "dread" the problem of getting rid of all that honey? It's a nice problem to have! Lots of beekeepers wished they had that problem.

This manuscript is about producing large crops of honey. I dream of making monster crops of honey, and I'm willing to do what needs to be done to make it so.

But I've never had any "dread" of how I was going to get rid of it. Really! How many of us would welcome that problem, and not see it as a problem but a wonderful opportunity?

And I've never had the mindset that I had to "get rid of it." There will always be a market for honey. Good, locally produced honey sells itself— maybe not all at once. But once people know you have good honey, they'll find you and you will not have to "get rid of it." Harvesting a monster crop of honey is a wonderful opportunity, and anything but a burden. As beekeepers, we ought to be looking forward to producing tons of honey.

In my mind, there's nothing more exciting than feeling the strain of my back and arms as I pry loose and hoist that heavy super of wall-to-wall honey from a hive frothing with bees. It is the dream of every beekeeper to have their preparation and hard work rewarded with multiple supers of solid frames of capped honey comb from every hive. I love to pull the fully-capped frame all nice and white with the wax covering that golden liquid underneath.

Extracting that honey crop is yet another dream, however. And let's face it, extracting is work. Sometimes it's kind of tedious work. And to some beekeepers, marketing and selling that honey may be a nightmare. Still, to get into that nightmare is something just about every beekeeper would gladly welcome.

But the reality is that you don't get into this situation by continuing to slap the managerial "snooze alarm," nor do you decide to wake up and start this process just as the honey flow starts. You need to prepare. You need to be proactive. Things need to be done in anticipation of the nectar flow. Everything is interrelated and integrated. This is where the rest of this manuscript is going to take you.

But I have to ask you: Are you willing to do the work it takes to get high honey yields? On one hand we look to successful beekeepers and say, "They are the luckiest people in the world." Sometimes, when someone shares their enthusiasm for all the honey they are harvesting, the lazy beekeepers scoff, "Yeah, he's just one lucky guy."

Really? Is that all it is? It's all just luck?

But what is luck? I see luck as ***opportunity meeting preparation.***

The "lucky" beekeepers were in position (because they prepared) to receive their fortunate circumstance (life's opportunity). They harvested a large amount of honey because they prepared for it and worked out a plan. When opportunity arose (like good weather and a strong nectar flow) they had their hives prepared with healthy, strong populations of foragers and ample supers in place ready to go.

The rest of us sat around, admiring the sunshine and warm weather wondering why we still have our boxes of frames and foundation in the basement workshop waiting to be put together, waiting for a moment when we could, "find the time." If this is your situation, I can guarantee you that you'll never **find** the time; you need to **take** the time after you **make** the time.

And while I cannot guarantee you the opportunities that bring you luck, I can, however, guarantee that if you're not prepared it doesn't matter what comes along: You're out of position and you're going to miss it.

And luck is not elusive nor is it exclusive. It's merely the right preparation awaiting the right opportunity. But if you don't prepare, then the opportunity is wasted. Then you'll probably blame "bad" luck for your lack of success.

As I said earlier, there are three kinds of beekeepers:

Those who make things happen.
Those who watch things happen.
Those who wonder what just happened.

I aim to be the first kind. And I know my share of beekeepers who feel that this hobby of ours is just too much work. I hear people tell me they want to enjoy their bees. They go on about how they just leave the bees alone and take what honey they give (if they give you any extra honey at all). And they don't worry about mites or disease or the timely application of miticides or medications.

But these "leave alone" beekeepers wake up one day and their bees are dead, or they starved in the middle of the winter, or they swarmed and absconded to parts unknown. Then they get frustrated and they put the equipment in the garage thinking that next year they'll just order another package.

Then next year turns into five years and nothing is accomplished. Then the wax moths find those frames of beautiful wax or the mice move in and chew up the super, and in the process, make a smelly little next in the dry comb.

I find this situation very sad. There was so much potential that was simply squandered in laziness and procrastination.

If you're one of these beekeepers, you need to read my other report, *"The Making of a Beekeeper."* I included it at the end of this manuscript. It explores the questions surrounding your motivation for keeping bees. I want to ask frankly, "Do you have what it takes to be a beekeeper?" Simply having some bees in a box in the backyard doesn't necessarily make you a beekeeper. Having nice new equipment doesn't make you a beekeeper either.

Many "wanna-be" beekeepers start out gloriously, but soon fail and quit. It's not easy doing what you have to do to successfully manage a colony of honeybees. Those who don't manage tend to be absentee landlords of wooden boxes and they soon quit when trouble strikes or their bees abscond. Most of our problems stem from irrational fears and a lack of will to do what needs to be done. I address these issues in that publication.

For those who continue in beekeeping, they might not necessarily want huge honey yields. I frequently hear the complaint, "But I don't know what to do with all that honey." My first response is, "Hey!

Sell it! Make some money. Get a return on your investment."

And sometimes my beekeeping buddies say, "But I'm not in it for the money."

Honey sales are the point of profitability for most beekeeping endeavors. You'll just have to find a way to sell it or make use of it. Having lots of honey is a nice problem to have, and a nice problem most beekeepers rarely encounter. You can always give it away if money is not your motive.

Heck, buy some small squeeze bottles and donate a couple cases of honey to the local food pantry. Or start getting creative with your marketing efforts. If you just want to keep bees, help your kids sell it door-to-door and let them keep the money. Set up a table of quart jars with a free-will offering jar at your church and give the money to the mission committee.

I can't help but emphasize that harvesting honey is a wonderful opportunity and not a burden. And honey will never spoil so storing it is a perfectly reasonable option. If you can't sell all of it right after the harvest, don't worry. Store it in a warm environment. Give it away as Christmas presents. Set up a table at the church bazaar.

And remember that you will harvest the majority of your honey in the July-August-September time frame. It's in the months of May and June that my supplies start to run out. And those are the months of the peak selling at the farmer's markets. I'm looking for a monster crop of honey that will last me from one year until I harvest the new crop the following year.

At this juncture let me tell you this fact: I have never had any problem selling my honey. People, once they know you have honey, will kick your door down to buy quality, locally-produced honey. If anything, I have to turn people away when my supplies are getting tight. Demand for my honey has always exceeded my supply. My goal is to produce as much honey as is possible. Selling it has never been a problem.

I even have other beekeepers call me wanting honey in five-gallon buckets because they sold all their honey and they can't meet their demand!

Now lots of beekeepers dream of making lots of _money_, but they don't want to work at making lots of _honey_. But you can't sell something you don't have. I can almost guarantee you that if you produce a ton of honey, the money will flow right along side of it.

However, if your bees don't produce a monster crop of honey, then you have nothing to worry about. And sadly, most beekeepers I know don't want to put in the time and effort it takes to produce these monster crops of honey. It's easier to leave the bees alone to do what they will, harvest what meager amounts they'll give you, then complain how this beekeeping is "nothing more than a rich man's hobby."

I don't have any problem finding ways to sell all my honey—and I sell out every year. The first years I started keeping bees, selling honey took a little creativity, a little bit of work which is called "marketing." But I'd rather face the problem of selling my honey than not having any honey to sell. The honey is my personal reward for treating my bees with respect and sound management. If there is no surplus honey, I can usually look to my lack of desire to do what needed to be done. Lack of will is also laziness because I didn't care enough to educate myself on what needed to be done.

Having seen my share of beekeepers come and go, and some that stayed gone, I was moved to write my publication called *"The Making of a Beekeeper."* It's something everyone who ever lit a smoker should read. Too many people start keeping bees thinking they have what it takes. Few, however, continue. Fewer still, find success. Some should have never started.

Are you one of former or the latter? It's not too late to get your head screwed on straight. Every year is a new beginning, but I hate to see these remedial beekeepers continue to repeat the first grade of beekeeping school.

There's enough opportunity to keep bees that no one needs to feel there are too many beekeepers in the business or that beekeeping is something left up to the professional. There are ample opportunities to sell honey. I hope you'll take time to read my little essay at the end of this manuscript and continue in your commitment to keep bees.

Management is Preparation:

If you want to maximize your honey production, several things must be in place prior to the honey flow. There are a couple of situations that must be in place the previous season, well before you put your bees to bed for the winter.

Planning is imperative. Preparation is mandatory. Good management anticipates what should happen and makes the adjustments ahead of time to catch the opportunity and avert the disaster. The opportunities will come. Make sure you are prepared. Luck, good fortune, big honey crops are nothing more than opportunity meeting preparation. You cannot control the opportunities, but you are definitely in charge of the preparation!

Success in beekeeping is not something that merely happens (although defining success is often personal and subjective—some people are merely satisfied with doing the least, hoping for the best and accepting what the bees offer). However, great honey harvests are no miracle, nor do they happen by accident. Success is the result of your good planning meeting the wealth of opportunity, but it also helps to be blessed by great weather and keeping your bees in an abundant location.

There are five major factors to maximizing your honey production, each of which plays a significant role. These five factors are 1) overwintering strong colonies; 2) getting a rapid spring build up; 3) preventing the swarming impulse; 4) supering intelligently; and 5) harvesting early and often.

I want to devote a single chapter to each of these five factors, respectively. Yet for now, I want to prepare you, the beekeeper, mentally as well as philosophically to get yourself ready to take on the challenge of implementing all five factors.

All five factors are important and work together in a cooperative role. They're synergistic. If you miss out on one of these factors, you'll miss out on achieving the maximum honey potential of your hive. Which doesn't mean you won't get by if you don't do all these things. It just means you won't achieve the best possible results or reach your maximum potential.

Sometimes the bees mystify our noblest objections and defy our well-intentioned excuses. They bring in a monster honey crop in spite of our protestations and despite our procrastinations. We forget the bees know more than we know.

Still, we are managers, "stewards," if you will, entrusted with their talent and instinct to gather nectar and the marvelous potential to make a ton of honey. All these factors fall into a situation and responsibility we call "management."

And quite frankly, we need to prepare ourselves before we even think about preparing our hives. Do we have what it takes? Are we, as beekeepers, mentally prepared to do what needs to be done, when it needs to be done, in order to maximize the colony's potential to gather nectar and turn it into honey?

Like any good athlete or a promising musician, are we willing to do the drills, practice the pieces to insure when it comes for the performance, we are at the top of our game?

Every Hive Has Potential:

I believe every colony has the potential to respond to sound management. This potential may not necessarily yield huge honey harvests, yet every hive can move beyond the "normal" potential to the higher levels with prudent management, visionary planning and timely execution of preparation meeting opportunity.

Some beekeepers will leave the bees alone and hope they get lucky. Luck, however, has very little to do with your habitual procrastination. Luck is all about preparation.

You're probably tired of me telling you luck is all about preparation. Actually, it's about being responsible to do what needs to be done. Unfortunately, responsibility is not something we naturally welcome into our lives. Still, monster honey crops hinge on our responsibility to prepare the hive and to prepare ourselves before the season starts.

And perhaps you're wondering, "Why all this hub-bub and hulabaloo about getting the maximum production from your hives? It sounds like TOO MUCH WORK!"

Well, it is a lot of work. But if you didn't put in the work, and if you didn't give your hive every opportunity to excel, how would you know what it's capable of doing? If you've been doing the wrong thing for years (and not knowing it was the wrong thing) how would you know your management (mismanagement) is actually holding your bees back?

The real problem with most beekeepers is that they go about doing the same thing every year because they don't see any differences. I talk to beekeepers all over the United States who are happy with 20, 30 or even 40 pounds of production, never knowing that 75, 100, 150 pounds are possible. And sometimes just changing one or two things can make a huge difference.

But you never know until you try. I've outlined the five most critical factors in my operation that made a night and day difference. Any one of them will make a difference, but they tend to build on each other. They complement each other. They strengthen each other. They balance each other. They say to one another, *"You complete me."* (Blatantly stolen from the movie, *Jerry McGuire.*)

Even if you don't achieve a harvest of 300 pounds per hive, these five factors will help your bees achieve their relative, maximum potential. And in reality, some hives or some breeds of bees are simply not prolific enough to produce record amounts of honey.

Still, follow these guidelines and you'll take advantage of the positive traits your bees possess and you can help them maximize their potential.

So how is it possible to maximize your hive's potential? At the outset, let me say that your knowledge and management skills are the two most critical factors you can control. Left alone, honeybees will do just fine bringing in an average, sustainable crop.

But if the mites are left unchecked and if the overcrowding that leads to swarming is not alleviated, the bees will not reach their potential. They may not even live. These are factors within your managerial control.

In the wild, without human intervention (or interference), it's not uncommon for a hive to produce 25 to 30 pounds of surplus honey in a good year. The bees survive the winter without supplemental feeding (because no one has greedily stolen too much honey) and since there is no outside help, they'll eat up these 25 to 30 pounds of honey over the winter.

Sadly, some of my own hives don't get this much surplus honey or do this well because I messed them up with my ignorant management practices.

Sometimes my ignorant management practices are not tough enough to cull out a poor queen or wise enough to simply concede that this weak hive needs to be consolidated into another weak hive. Like other beekeepers, I draw a certain pride from saying that I have a certain number of hives.

But your management can play a significant role in maximizing their potential. Consider how a healthy hive responds normally to the forces of nature. When the weather warms up, the queen lays more eggs. When the plants bloom, they gather nectar. But the bees don't take into account the anticipation of the honey flow and maximize what could be possible.

Bees work based on what the day holds. They don't stop and think about what could be done if they planned ahead.

That's your role as the beekeeper. You need to plan and anticipate and offer them the resources they need to maximize their potential. Honeybees will do what they need to do to survive, but a good manager can work with their instinctive skills and produce larger than "normal" crops of honey.

And all of the requirements for maximum honey harvests must be in place BEFORE the honey flow, and sadly, most beekeepers find themselves "asleep at the switch" and your maximum honey crop is just a fantasy dream.

Let's take a look at each of these factors, and if you are finding yourself behind schedule this year and unable to get ready, then you need to make the best of this year and make your plans for next year's honey crop.

Ironically, the first factor takes place this year, in anticipation of next year. So it may be too late, or this first factor may be something you're already doing.

You also need to know when your honey flow comes on, which for most of us happens around late April into early July, with minor flows in September when it starts to rain, and this schedule varies from year to year, region to region. Weather is the big wild card in the beekeeping business.

Most larger beekeepers keep an old-fashioned scale with a hive on it. They measure the weight of the hive every night, after all the field bees are in for the night. When they see a jump of 15 to 20 pounds in a day, the honey flow is on! Since the date for this time varies every year, a scale is a great idea to affirm when you need to give your bees your utmost attention.

Maximum honey production depends on your ability to have all five factors in place before the honey flow starts so you can ride out the weather extremes. If you can't get these five factors accomplished, then you need to give up your hopes of a maximum honey crop. You'll have to settle for what you get and hope for great weather to pull off a decent crop despite your inability, laziness, busyness or distractions that keep you from getting your bees in shape.

These five factors require discipline on your part, and some people just don't want these kinds of details to get in the way of their other activities. You hold the future of your success in your hands.

There is an old story about a wise old man in a village. He was the local elder to whom many people turned to for answers to their problems. An envious young man didn't care for the attention given to the wise old man so he devised a scheme that would prove the old man was nothing but a fool.

The young man took a pigeon and tucked the pigeon's head under its own wing so it would remain motionless. Holding the bird behind his back, the young man would ask the wise old man if the bird was alive or dead. If the wise old man answered, "Dead," then the young man would flip the bird into the air, untucking its head in the process, and it would fly away.

If the old man answered, "Alive," then the young man would continue to hold the bird behind his back and gently, but forcefully, squeeze the bird and kill it instantly. Either way the young man felt he could not lose and the old man could not win. Then the villagers would note how the young man was the wisest person in the village.

The day came and the young man approached the wise old man. Holding the pigeon behind his back, asking the question, if the bird was alive or dead, the young man felt he had cornered the wise old man and finally shown the village who was truly the wisest. And so he posed his question to the old man, "Is the bird I hold behind my back alive or is it dead?"

The wise old man thought for a moment and said, "That question has more than one answer, but this one thing I know: You hold that answer to the question in your own hands." And the young man knew he had been outsmarted and quietly left.

When it comes to beekeeping, you hold the answer to your future in your own hands. Will your hives produce a record crop and fulfill their fullest potential, or will they only do the best they can given limiting circumstances because you neglected them?

The answer lies in your own hands. How you deal with your bees, how well you anticipate their needs, how much you prepare to meet the expected opportunity will determine the answer to that question. You hold your future in your own hands.

Large harvests of honey are easily within your grasp. But whether or not they become a reality is something you hold in your own hands, and it's called management.

Addendum to Chapter 3:

Plan Ahead

This is an addendum to chapter 3. It's called "Plan Ahead." You have to remember that it wasn't raining when Noah built the ark. And good beekeepers don't wait until spring before they start assembling their equipment. And the best beekeepers insure they order the necessary equipment prior to the seasonal demands.

Here's my advice: plan ahead; order early; be prepared.

My busiest time is winter. While it's cold outside and the bees are nestled tightly in their hives, I'm in my heated workshop assembling frames and painting hives. Everything needs to be ready to go prior to the warmth of spring. Once spring arrives, time is short and I don't want to fall behind trying to get stuff ready.

Another thing I need to keep in mind: when it's cold, the suppliers will not ship wax foundation. Wax foundation is brittle in the cold and it breaks. So all my wax foundation needs to be ordered in the fall. How much will I need? I don't really know! Now I need to anticipate my needs, or worse, guess at what might be expected.

What I have done over the years is to keep a ready supply of all supplies on hand the year round. My workshop is like a small beekeeping supply company. I keep shelves filled with inventory, and when my supplies run low, I reorder BEFORE I run out.

I don't want to run out of anything, and it seems I usually run out at the same time demand is the highest. As an example, in the spring, EVERYONE wants frames and foundation, packages and queens. In the summer, EVERYONE wants plastic squeeze bottles for the farmer's markets. The best time or order supplies is when no one else wants them. Yes, you may have to store them until the seasonal demand, but you'll sleep better at night knowing your supply is ready for you when your need arises.

I have spent too many years of my younger life living a day late and a dollar short. I've noted seasonal demands (usually when prices are highest and supplies scarce) and I've noted when seasonal lulls bring on specials and close-outs (when suppliers want to move their left-over inventory). So I buy a lot of my supplies in the fall in anticipation of spring

Yeah, there have been times I ordered in the spring only to have my desperately needed supplies put on a 30-day "back order." Now that does me a lot of good! So my advice is this: Order when no one else wants anything, and even if it's back ordered, you'll get it in plenty of time. Yet if you wait until peak demand drains the supplier's inventory, you are at their mercy.

My wife is the same way. She shops for Christmas decorations on December 26th in anticipation of the next Christmas. She buys left-over Valentine decorations on February 15th. Now the variety is not always plentiful, but she makes up for it with the bargains and she's ready to go for the next year.

So here's just a little piece of advice: When you desperately need a specific, seasonal item, so will every beekeeper in the country. Order early. Take delivery during slow times. There are ample stories in different cultures about how the ant worked during the hot summer while the grasshopper played and relaxed. When winter came, the ant was snug with ample food and the grasshopper was left to starve.

The bees seem to know this same principle. Beekeepers ought to have it figured out by now as well. Plan ahead. Be prepared. Have the supplies you need before you need them. Then listen to all your grasshopper buddies complain how they need foundation for all those swarm calls they're getting.

Chapter 4: Overwinter Strong Colonies

The First Factor

As I said in the previous chapter, I want to devote a single chapter to each of the respective five factors in producing the maximum amount of honey each colony is capable of producing.   I want each colony to live up to its potential.

Beekeeping is harder than one really imagines. Some beekeepers leave their bees alone and let them "fend for themselves" or "let nature take her course." This is the first level: the leave them alone approach. And with this approach, the bees will normally survive, but produce only enough to sustain themselves.

Maybe.

The next level up from this attitude is to reduce all the limiting factors that prevent the bees from making great honey yields. And if you merely removed the impediments, the bees will do wonderfully well, and much better than if you did nothing. This is the second level: **the remove the challenges approach**. And with this approach, the bees will produce a modest surplus, but it's going to have to be a good year.

But to really get ahead, to really harvest the honey crop your bees were built and programmed to bring in, you cannot merely just take away the limitations. You need to implement the proactive factors that will allow your bees to live up to their potential. This is the third level: **to provide the resources the bees really need to enhance their natural instincts approach**. This is the approach you'll need to take if you want to harvest those monster crops of honey.

This chapter is about the first factor in taking those proactive steps toward harvesting those monster honey crops.

Strong Colonies:

The first factor in managing your hives for maximum production is to have a strong colony. You definitely want a strong colony in the early spring. A strong colony in the spring will produce a greater population of foragers, which in turn, brings in more nectar which produces more honey.

Now here's the catch. A queen lays an egg and it takes three weeks until it hatches into a worker bee. That's three weeks you'll need to wait.

Okay, that worker bee emerges from its pupal cell and will spend the next three weeks working around the hive, feeding larvae, drawing out wax for comb building, etc. We call these young workers "house" bees or "nurse" bees. So for the next three weeks, these bees will not bring in any nectar. They just take care of the hive.

After these three weeks (it's now six weeks after the queen has laid the egg) these house bees mature into foragers. Sometimes we call these bees "field" bees. Their duty is to gather the nectar and pollen.

And if you do the math, you need the queen laying eggs AT LEAST six weeks prior to the nectar flow in order to have a sustainable work force gathering nectar. The more, the better. The earlier, the better. You need to build up your colony's population just as early as you possibly can so you can have a large army of field bees to forage for nectar and pollen.

And here's the key point: these foragers have to be in place six weeks before the nectar flow starts. You want a hive to get up and running as early in the spring as you can, and you need a queen that will start laying eggs as early as possible in order to experience a population growth ahead of the nectar flow.

Now some of this population growth will be governed by the weather, but the key to having a strong spring population is to create the optimal situations to develop a strong fall population going into winter.

One of the ideals that foster a strong spring build-up is to bring a hive into the winter months with a strong population. Most beekeepers are only thinking about surviving the winter, or at least preparing the hive for the winter. I'm thinking about getting the colony stronger in the fall, hoping the queen will lay more eggs late in the season! Younger bees survive the winter better than older bees.

When does a strong winter population start? In August and September.

One of the tricks to having a strong colony in the spring is to overwinter a strong colony from the previous fall. And just as a side note, strong fall populations going into the winter will also need a generous supply of winter stores. If they don't have honey, you'll need to feed them supplemental syrup. Also, a pollen substitute patty will be of benefit in the fall and winter months as well.

Beekeeping really begins in the fall. I like to think of my "new year" as beginning on August 1st. If I get everything done that I want to get done, all my honey is harvested by August 1st and I shift from my honey production to spring preparations that create a strong colony when the weather breaks the following year.

Now most people can't envision this scenario. But in order to have a strong colony in the spring, you need a healthy, strong colony going into winter. Since honeybees don't simply switch gears and magically produce more workers, you need to back up from the winter months to the early fall months to get this strong, healthy population of honeybees ready for the winter.

This is the first factor for monster honey crops: bring a strong population of honeybees, preferably as young as possible, through the winter into the spring. And winter management really begins in August and September.

And that's hard to get into my thick skull. I'm sweating in the hot, humidity of an August afternoon and I'm trying to tell myself I'm getting ready for January. It just doesn't make sense!

So on August 1st I begin my mite treatments. I requeen my colonies with young, enthusiastic, egg-laying queens. I start feeding high-protein diets to encourage those young queens to produce a new generation of young bees (again, let me repeat: young bees are more apt to survive the winter than old bees). All my fall preparations will become apparent in April the next year. All my procrastinations will be revealed next April as well!

Unfortunately, the average beekeeper who wants a strong colony in April starts thinking about strong colonies in April rather than August. Sometimes I get calls in the month of April from new beekeepers who want to add a pollen substitute to boost the queen's eagerness to lay more eggs. I usually give them some kindly advice, but in reality, they're about two months too late. They need to get those pollen substitute patties on earlier. Winter would have been ideal, the late fall even better.

Typically, however, we can't get into our hives (due to weather and coldness) until mid-March. By this time, the bees are already foraging fresh pollen and a pollen substitute is probably not needed. It should have been added back in January, but since the weather is really too cold to manage hives in January, this work needs to be done earlier.

So I find myself adding pollen substitute patties in December before the weather really turns cold here in southeast Missouri. But in reality, if I could get into my bee yards, I can still open the top cover, remove the inner cover, add a patty and close up the hive without doing too much damage to the bees.

One spring, probably in March, I got out into one of my fields to find a hive with the top completely blown off. The bricks that held down the outer cover were on the ground, and next to it, the outer cover and the inner cover. The top hive body and all the frames were exposed to the elements. I expected the worst, but there, humped and hunched over the comb, shivering to keep warm, was the cluster of honeybees. I replaced the lid and the colony survived into the spring and summer.

I was amazed. So don't get too uppity or worrisome about lifting off a lid in the cold of January to put on a pollen patty. The bees will survive. Add the pollen patties well before the bees have access to naturally occurring pollen. The thought is once natural pollen is available, the bees won't take a pollen substitute. This is partly true. I buy, and I have made pollen substitutes that are enhanced with additives to encourage consumption (specifically, Honey-B-Healthy). The point is to get that protein supplement on the bees as soon as you can.

Beekeeping is largely the result of your proactive management. You need to give the bees what they need before they know they need it. So once my honey is harvested in July, I start making plans to build my colonies for the following spring around the first part of August. I want a strong colony in the spring and it starts with a strong colony going into winter. Strong winter colonies begin in August.

Strong colonies with large populations of worker bees produce large amounts of honey. Most of us want a strong colony about the first week in May when the weather *really* moderates favorably (at least here in southeast Missouri) and we can see the clover begin to blossom.

Based on my experience, I can tell you this: a strong, over-wintered colony will out-produce a nuc or a package, even a nuc or package settled into an old dead-out hive with drawn comb. There is something magical about bringing that colony through the winter with a young queen and a robust population of bees. And in the spring, that strong, over-wintered colony is the thing you want.

So one of my main goals is to give my hives lots of Tender Loving Care in August. Honeybees respond quite favorably to sound management. Unfortunately, this is when most beekeepers are tired of extracting. It's hot and humid. The bees tend to be a little rambunctious.

However, the seeds of sound management, sown in August, bear much fruit when April rolls around. I will do everything in my power to insure my hives are strong, healthy and loaded with sufficient feed going into the winter months. But winter management is really fall management. You need to be proactive. You need to plan ahead.

So strong colonies begin in August, nine months before you really want those colonies to be in peak condition by April. There are three things to do in August to get a strong colony in the spring, and a fourth if your hives are small and these first three don't seem to work.

First, requeen. Simply put, young queens outlay old queens and young queens reduce the swarming impulse. Requeening in August is a better deal than waiting for spring. I'll have more to say on this in a minute.

Second, treat for mites and disease at this time. By August in southeast Missouri, most of our honey crop is in and harvested. Some beekeepers wait until Labor Day, but for the most part, we're done with the honey harvest by August. With the honey off the hive, it's now safe to treat for mites and disease. Plus, some of the treatments are temperature sensitive, such as menthol treatments for tracheal mites, or any of the thymol-based varroa treatments. Treat your hives in August for a healthy hive next spring.

If a hive is stressed with mites or disease, it won't stand the rigors of the winter as well as a treated hive and will likely die out. Then you'll be asking me, "So what do you think they died of?" My response will normally be, "Neglect and procrastination."

Third, feed, feed, feed. I like to take off lots of honey and feed syrup. While lots of beekeepers cringe at the cost (and labor) of feeding supplemental syrup, I can sell my honey for ten times what syrup costs to replace the harvested honey. I can also treat the syrup with medication, if necessary, or even add some protein supplement like MegaBee or Honey-B-Healthy.

Feeding the bees at this time also helps, as August offers no good nectar sources here in southeast Missouri. If August is hot and dry, September will not offer much in terms of fall flowers for the bees to gather nectar (like goldenrod). By feeding in August, I want the queen to think the nectar flow is still on and keep laying eggs. I want a good strong colony going into winter.

And if three fourths of the bees in each hive will die during the winter months, I need a lot of bees, especially young bees, going into winter to have a nice population at the first warm break in the spring. Feeding also insures that I'll have ample stores for winter survival. The time to feed is when the weather is warm and the bees can store and ripen the nectar/syrup.

Of course, this also means you won't be able to harvest any "fall" honey (as it's mixed with treated sugar syrup), but it will be a small price to pay when you consider the abundant crop next year. And in southeast Missouri, our fall honey flow is very fickle and undependable. I don't even bother to mess with it. It's easier to simply let the bees keep it all.

In August, take your honey and feed, or feed to insure good winter stores. Don't wait and hope for fall honey. I've been caught in late October with low stores of honey and you simply cannot force enough syrup on the bees to do any good. The syrup is just too dilute. If short, you can successfully fend off starvation by feeding candy boards, fondant, or even dry sugar. But ideally, feed ahead of time, let the bees store it, and you'll gain the dividends next spring.

Fourth, combine weak colonies. There is a saying among successful beekeepers: "Take your losses in the fall and make your increases in the spring."

What they mean is a single strong hive will more likely survive the winter than two weak hives. You are better off combining hives, losing a couple of weak hives in the process to make one hive that will be strong enough to winter through, than if you left several smaller colonies to try and make it on their own. One strong hive will survive better than two weak hives, if they survive at all.

And I can't tell you how often I've been too stubborn and too greedy to do what needed to be done. I stupidly resisted combining weak hives. If the fall is dry and nectar scarce, if the winter turns cold and nasty, I'm going to have a bunch of dead bees. That's when I make that promise that I will not allow a weak colony to try and struggle against an impossible winter. I'm always better off combining, even letting the respective queens fight it out, than leaving two weak hives to die.

The secret to strong hives in the spring is to create the opportunity that makes for strong, populous hives of healthy bees in the fall. Not only do more warm bodies keep the hive warm, and dry, through the winter, but strong colonies also have enough bees to generate enough heat in the cool spring for successful brood rearing. If there are not enough bees to cluster and keep the brood warm, then the queen will wait until the weather moderates before she begins to lay eggs in earnest. The earlier eggs are laid, the earlier you will have a large work force to gather lots of nectar. The larger the work force, the more nectar will be gathered and your honey production increases. These numbers go hand-in-hand.

Strong hives going into the winter can be split in the spring, but smaller, weaker hives in which the queen is waiting for decent spring weather will not be large enough to split. So combine hives in the fall and take your "losses." Bring a strong hive through the winter, and if you want to make splits or increases, order yourself some queens for the spring and make yourself some splits. But if you leave weak hives in the fall, they won't be strong enough to split in the spring, provided they survive the winter.

Let me also digress for a moment. I like to make my splits in August when I requeen. The prevailing, conventional wisdom suggests the time for making splits is in the spring. I had a host of bad queens purchased from early, southern producers.

And I'm not sure it was the producer's fault as much as it was the cold, wet weather when they were trying to mate those queens. I had so many bad, poorly-mated mail-order queens that I started raising my own queens. However, I can't raise early queens in Southeast Missouri. So I raise summer queens for fall (August) splits.

As I shifted to summer queens, I noticed that when I didn't split my hives in the spring, these hives produced large crops of honey. Now splitting is a fine way to prevent swarms, but a spring split will not produce near the honey as an "unsplit" hive. Split hives won't swarm nearly so much, but they won't produce as much honey. On the other hand, you have two colonies when you split them rather than the one strong colony. But two split hives cannot produce as much as a single, "unsplit" hive.

So what I do is overwinter a strong colony, then work to prevent swarming in the spring (which is another chapter coming up) and make my splits in August. Further, something I discovered, is that if I split my hives in the spring, I have the potential to produce two hives from the one original hive. Summer splits produce eight to ten hives from that same original hive. The summer hives just have more bees and more brood. If fed, these summer splits continue to grow under favorably warm conditions. And the weather is ALWAYS more favorable in the summer than in the early spring.

If you purchase queens from a queen producer, you'll find summer queens to be cheaper and of higher quality than the early spring queens.

But I digress. My point is to keep strong colonies strong in the spring if you want to harvest monster crops of honey. You can make splits later in the summer to increase the number of your hives.

Before we move on to the other factors for maximizing your honey yields, let me add some more details to these four aspects of creating a strong hive for the winter.

Requeen

First, requeen, and I do it in August or September. Most conventional beekeepers say, "What? In August? Why not wait until spring when we're *supposed* to requeen?"

Who said you were supposed to requeen in the spring? Who said this was the only way?

Most beekeepers will make splits and requeen in the spring. Southern-bred queens are available in the spring (but this is also the time when everybody wants them, too—and they are more expensive). But why is this the time to do it? Commercial honey producers do it as they make splits, but not every hive I have needs to be split, nor am I a conventional, commercial beekeeper in the sense that there is only one way to do things.

Commercial beekeepers, as a general practice, make splits to retard the swarming impulse, and swarming can be a problem for the commercial beekeeper because he or she doesn't have the time to devote to every hive and use alternative means to prevent swarming. For the commercial beekeeper, it is better to make a split (which will still be moderately productive) than to lose a hive's potential honey crop to swarming. It's mostly about timing.

And since commercial beekeepers can't give every hive the same TLC that a smaller beekeeper provides, making spring splits is a good way to fill the empty boxes from winter dead-outs.

I will make my splits in July and August on really strong hives. I will also requeen hives in August as it's easier and more convenient than waiting until spring. Also, I've had so many poorly mated queens that didn't work out in the spring that I've gone to fall requeening to make sure they'll do what they're supposed to do. This way, with fall requeening, I get to test my queens and insure their quality, and I insure they'll be accepted.

I favor fall requeening. If I choose to buy a queen, they're cheaper in the summer/fall than spring queens when EVERYBODY wants a queen. I also believe the fall queens have better breeding because they have a greater selection of drones to mate with. However, not all queen breeders have fall queens available. For this reason, I've gone to raising my own queens (and believe me, it ain't that hard to raise your own queens and you don't have to graft larvae if you don't want to).

To requeen in the spring is dependent upon good weather to introduce the queen, plus dependent upon the queen breeder's ability to produce quality queens that are well mated (also weather dependent). Then you also have cold weather when the queens are shipped. If I were to buy spring queens, I would buy them from some place warm, like Hawaii. Still, those queens have to be shipped in unpredictable weather.

Further, the colony's inclination to accept the queen depends upon the weather as queens are more readily accepted during a honey flow. Springtime weather has a habit of sending us a solid week of cold, damp drizzle that impedes good acceptance. I've ordered spring queens only to have to hold them in my basement for a week while I waited for good weather. Then I've also got some bee yards that turn to slick mud during the wet spring weather. Gaining access to my hives to requeen is a problem.

Queens are better accepted if there is a nectar flow happening. Fall (September) has a minor flow, but I also feed my bees a 1:1 syrup and Honey-B-Healthy to insure queen acceptance when I introduce them. The cold weather in spring also makes it harder for the bees to break from the cluster and get to the feed.

Using standard methods of queen introduction (still in the mailing cage and allowing them to eat the candy plug) requires four to seven days in which there are no eggs laid. I can't afford seven days in the spring when no eggs are laid. I've tried to speed the process up by clearing a hole in the candy plug with a nail.

But lately I've changed my mind on this idea. I have found that when I rush the queen's emergence from the queen cage, the colony allows this strange queen to lay a few eggs. Then they kick her out and turn these eggs into supersedure cells.

Then I've really found myself up a creek with no paddles and a leaking boat. That new queen in the supersedure cell needs sixteen days to emerge, then four to seven days to mate, then a few more days before she lays eggs. I can end up with four weeks of no production before she starts laying eggs. Those eggs need six weeks (three weeks to emerge, three weeks as a house bee) before they become bees ready to gather nectar. With spring introduction, I may miss the honey flow all together if the queen doesn't work out.

Let me just say, at this point, that I now simply remove the cork on a queen cage to expose the candy plug. I don't open the hole with a nail. If the queen takes a couple of days longer to get out, so much the better. She's accepted better if they have a chance to acclimate themselves to her smell. Still, I've lost the time in which she could be laying eggs. In the fall, these days of lost egg production are not so important.

Let me also add that if you buy your replacement queens, find a queen breeder that offers the genetic resistance to diseases. These queens are sometimes called SMR or VSH and are noted as having "hygienic behavior." More and more queen breeders are raising their bees without chemicals and that's a bonus as well.

I'm also becoming more convinced that it is better to raise your own queens from your own locally-adapted stock. Raising your own queens is not hard, or at least not as hard as you might think it is, but it's really a subject for another day.

Treat for Mites and Disease:

Second, treat for mites and disease. I've already alluded to the fact that certain treatments, such as menthol, require warmer temperatures to be effective. August and September are ideal months for menthol treatments. Treatment at this time is also advantageous because it's very likely your honey should be harvested and you have no risk of contaminating your honey, even with these organic, food-grade treatments.

Another good reason to treat at this time is the timing of mite populations. Particularly with varroa mites, their population tends to hold steady through the summer months. Then in August through October, the mite population in each hive tends to peak. These months are the best time to treat.

Winter months bring stresses of cold and humid hive conditions. Often, it is not the varroa that cause a bee to die. It is the weakened bee that is susceptible to opportunistic bacterial and viral diseases.

And I can tell you how I failed to treat hives that looked good and strong in June and July. I was too cheap and the bees looked too good to have varroa. But I had no idea on how to honestly assess if I had a problem or not. Later in the fall, or even during the winter, the whole colony died. All around them were ample stores of honey. As I cleaned the bottom board, I could see the dead varroa mites sprinkled among the dead bee bodies.

Since that time, I've also gone to screen bottom boards. These bottom boards help reduce mites and help increase ventilation. The increased ventilation helps moderate the humidity, which in turn lowers the disease incidence. What I've also learned is that it is far better to work to prevent diseases than be forced to treat. With bees, it is better to prevent problems than be forced to cure problems.

I expect to treat in the fall, but let me also give a warning to the problems that are developing because of our callously routine, prophylactic treatments. As we treat over and over, with the same chemicals, we are helping these parasitic organisms to develop a selective resistance to our treatments. The more chemicals we dump into our hives, the stronger the problems become. The stronger the problems mean we need stronger chemicals in the future. It becomes what the industry has called, "the chemical treadmill" that keeps going faster and faster.

I highly encourage treatment for mites and diseases. But do what you can to ascertain if you have conditions that warrant treatment. Not only is this a good thing to do to keep the mites and diseases from building resistance, it makes good economic sense. If you can determine if you have no problems with mites or disease, don't waste your money on useless treatments.

Personally, I've gone to more natural responses to treating bees for diseases and battling the mites. I like formic acid, an organic treatment. Formic acid is also temperature dependent. But how you go about treating mites naturally is an issue for another day. The point I want to drive home is to treat for mites and treat while the weather is suitable.

Feed to Insure Winter Survival:

Third, feed. Feeding at this time serves many purposes. First, it helps insure winter survival. Ample stores is the most important key to overwintering success. More hives starve to death (and often starve in February or March). Since I like to harvest my honey aggressively, I also create the possibility of starving if I don't feed additional syrup at this time. And yes, there are those who like to debate the merits of honey over sugar syrup, but I'm not going to go there now. That's a topic for another day.

Second, feeding at this time allows for the addition of medication or miticides, or if you are like me, the inclusion of essential oils to take a more natural approach. Lately I've felt the inclusion of Honey-B-Healthy and MegaBee protein supplements have been good for my bees. Now they cost more money and require more labor to feed, but I feel the addition of supplements to the syrup have been well-received and beneficial to the bees.

Third, feeding at this time keeps the queen interested in raising brood. Younger bees are more likely to survive the winter than older bees, but if you have more bees you have more mouths to feed and you need ample stores. It's a vicious circle. And there are some queens reputed to slow down in the late summer or early fall. The Carniolan breed is thought to do this, but a young Carniolan queen in a colony fed syrup will be induced to lay eggs.

August and September are great months to feed supplemental syrup as our fall honey flow is very unpredictable. We'll have some honey produced, but it is not good for human consumption (golden rod honey is down-right nasty). The warmer weather allows the bees to cure the syrup into honey. This is a good time to feed.

Combine Weak Hives:

Fourth, combine weak hives. I already spoke to this issue earlier. If everything else doesn't produce a growing population of strong bees, combine two weak colonies. The newspaper method of combining works best, and many times I don't even remove old queens (unless they are obviously worn out as indicated by their brood pattern).

Mostly, the hives I combine have been my late swarms. I take a lot of swarm calls and do a fair number of "cut outs." Some of the earlier swarms work out great, but the later ones just don't have the motivation to survive the winter.

If I chose not to requeen them with a known queen I raised or purchased, then I'll simply take the lid off a hive and cover it with a newspaper. Then I'll lift another weak hive off of its bottom board and put it on top. I end up with some confused bees and some odd configurations of brood boxes and honey supers, but you can sort these out later.

The newspaper method allows the bees to familiarize themselves with each other and fighting is reduced. I let the queens work it out from there, but I've also opened some hives in the spring and found two queens in the same area. (I mark all my queens so I knew they were from the previous colonies).

Most of my weaker hives are from smaller, later swarms I catch or trap with bait hives and pheromone lures. But a good question to ask is why this colony is a weak hive? Later swarms (like in late June or July) never really have the nectar flow to raise good brood. I feed syrup to most of my late swarms as a general practice. But if they are still small and if the queen hasn't laid well, then I'll go ahead and kill her. Chances are good she was not well mated anyway. Perhaps she was the older queen that needs to be superseded. Late swarms are also very susceptible to infestations of small hive beetles. Formic acid is a good method of ridding your hives of small hive beetles, but the temperatures for its application are more critical.

I'll monitor these swarms for mites using a screen bottom board and a sticky board underneath to catch the mite fall. Most of my swarms are free of mites, but for some reason, they just don't build up. Sometimes they just can't get the momentum going to raise a strong population of bees. With any swarm, the age of the queen is always in question. It takes the younger bees to raise brood, and if the swarm was comprised of older bees, then this queen doesn't really stand a chance even if she was a virgin when the swarm left.

I cannot stress how important it is to have a strong colony going into the winter months. Not only do strong colonies maintain their own health, but the extra bodies help keep early brood warm. We all want strong colonies when the nectar begins to flow. Strong spring colonies begin with strong colonies in the fall. August is the time in southeast Missouri to requeen, treat for diseases and mites, then feed for ample stores and combine if the hive is weak. Obviously, your seasonal schedule will vary accordingly.

If you can bring a strong colony through the winter, you'll have a better chance at developing a massive army of foraging field bees in the spring. This massive army requires a rapid spring build up and this is the topic of the next chapter.

The first factor toward your goal of harvesting maximum crops of honey is to begin with a strong, overwintered colony. Always keep in mind that beekeeping really begins in the fall. Winter management is really fall management.

Addendum to Chapter 4

Go With Your Strengths

If you had a normal year, you'll have a normal distribution of hives. You'll probably have 20% of your hives that are really strong, 20% that are nominally weak and unproductive, and the middle 60% that are pretty good to around "average."

My goal is to get those 60% that are average into that upper tier of production, but I find myself spending a lot of time with those lower, slower 20%.

Basically, I typically end up investing too many resources into those lower 20% and the return on my investment hardly justifies the risks I'm taking. One of those risks is my neglect of my top producing hives.

If I have a limited amount of time and energy, where is the best place to invest that time and energy? Obviously, my best bet is with my stronger hives.

One day I woke up and realized my best return comes from working with the top 20% first, then the middle 60%. The lower 20% usually didn't respond no matter what I did. They never produced any honey that warranted the time I invested with them. And this is the reality with some hives. No matter how much you try and work with them, they just don't respond.

So my advice is to work with your strongest, most productive hives. Go with your strengths.

Back in the old days, I seemed to spend a lot of time working with my weaker hives. Over the years, when I had a "laying worker," I'd spend an inordinate amount of time trying to get the colony requeened and back on track.

What did I have to show for my efforts? Nothing. The colony would never take a new queen, and if I finally got one installed, there wasn't enough time to get things organized before the fall. The colony was just too weak.

What do I do today? I let them dwindle down to nothing. I write them off. They take too many resources (time and energy) and there is seldom any pay-off. Weak colonies are a drain on my resources, as well. "Dinks," as we call them, for whatever reason, just can't seem to get organized and move forward. But there is still a great part of me that wants to help them along. Eventually, if they plod along, I'll requeen them or use them as a mating nuc.

If you believe the "Pareto Principle," 80% of your hives will only produce 20% of your total production. And likewise, 20% of your hives will account for 80% of your production. So which hives ought we to be working with and managing for higher production? Those top 20%, of course!

But which hives take up most of our time? The other 80%, of course.

I have heard another statistic that 5% of any given entity will bring in 50% of the production. So out of that 20% that bring in the 80% of the production, 5% will account for 50% and the remaining 15% will account for 30%

To put it in a tabular form:

5% of the hives	50% of the production
15% of the hives	30% of the production
80% of the hives	20% of the production

I've never really tested this idea, but I like its logic. If I believe the logic, then which hives should I be working with? The top producers!

Here is a little piece of advice: Go with your strengths. Keep your best management on the strongest, best-looking hives you got. Don't totally ignore the rest of your hives, but recognize your "bread and butter" hives will be those strong ones. Don't waste needless time and effort on those hives that won't pan out. Concentrate on your star pupils.

Which brings me back to something I said at the outset. There are two ways to bring in a huge honey crop. One way is to bring all your hives up to their potential. The other way is to simply keep more hives. Ten hives properly managed may produce the same amount of honey as thirty marginal hives. What counts for me is the total honey crop, but I also recognize the need to keep all my hives working toward loftier production goals.

And every year I have marginal hives that just don't produce very much. I don't pay much attention to them and I find they are stronger and more productive the next year—likely because they superseded that bum queen. It's kind of like they lay fallow for one year to gain the strength for the next year (kind of like apple trees that produce good crops on alternating years).

I seem to keep a lot of hives that don't really produce every year, but I keep them nonetheless. I'll requeen or use these hives for splits for my home-grown queens. I believe all hives bring a little bit of production to the table, but I don't squander too many resources trying to coax them along. There's an old expression about "whipping a dead horse." No matter how hard you whip it, it's not going to run any faster.

My hives are in a continual winnowing process of attrition of the weakest. Which is another way of saying survival of the fittest. I raise queens from hives that flourish under my management, and those that don't generally get winnowed out. And likewise, as I go about making new splits every year and raising new queens, there are always some hives that won't produce. It's a fact of beekeeping.

Go with your strengths. Dance with the girls that bring you to the ball. Don't waste your time on things that just won't pan out.

Chapter 5: Rapid Spring Build Up

The Second Factor

So our first factor is to bring a strong hive through the winter months and that idea begins with prudent preparations in the fall. Okay, now it's spring. Now what?

The second factor for maximum honey yields is to get the colony to shift from winter mode into a rapid spring build up. And the sooner this takes place in the late winter, the better.

What is desired in the second factor is a rapid spring build up from the winter population. I want a group of bees that are ready to go out and harvest nectar and pollen just as soon as the days are warm enough to coax those blooms to open.

And the key to high honey yields is having this population in place and ready to go **before** the nectar flow commences. This means you are asking your queen to start laying early and often, well before the normal seasonal cues tell her to start. One of the tips I'm going to offer, and it's fairly conventional wisdom, is to present the colony with pollen substitute and stimulative feeding of 1:1 syrup. More on this later.

I think the key to this second factor comes back to the idea that bees need time to develop. If you recall your honey bee biology, and let me remind you again, when worker bees emerge from their brood cells, they spend the first 21 days of their life housekeeping and tending to the needs of the larvae.

We often call these bees "house" bees or "nurse" bees. Their duties are pretty much confined to the hive for the next three weeks. As they mature during these three weeks, they'll also build comb, cap cells, ripen nectar and guard the front entrance from intruders. But for 21 days after emergence, they gather no nectar.

And also bear in mind, it takes 21 days just for them to mature from egg to nurse bee. Add those 21 days of gestation to the 21 days of nurse bee duty when they simply hang out in the hive and you have 42 days required to get that egg up to foraging ability. That's six weeks minimum of time you need to have a queen laying eggs and building a work force that will be mature enough to forage blooms.

Six weeks! And this is all before the nectar flow starts. I can't help but accentuate the reality of those six weeks.

Then once the worker bee starts foraging, she'll only live another two or three weeks, maybe four weeks until she works herself to death. The time will come when she takes that last load of nectar on a weakened body with tattered wings. The load will prove to be too much and she'll crash into the grass and die of exposure. You need a prolific queen and a continual succession of eggs laid each day to replace those dying bees.

Lots of young bees eventually become that mighty force of foragers. And this succession has to begin long before the blooms first appear. Ideally, it should come at a minimum of at least, at a very minimum, six weeks before the major honey flow.

And if you can get that queen to do it even earlier, so much the better!

As an example, if you want a work force to start gathering nectar and pollen on the first of April, this foraging bee must be "born" three weeks earlier on March 11th. While April 1st seems early, consider this is just the first day that the first wave of worker bees will be out foraging. Yes, it's early. But plants are in bloom in April, particularly several trees. By the first week in April, the dandelions begin to bloom. Shortly after that, the apple trees start blooming.

Consider this as well: this foraging bee is just the first of many generations of foraging bees you'll need when the honey flow comes on with real intensity (for our area, late April into late June, maybe even into early July). April 1st is a good target date to send out the first wave of field bees (at least for my area). Secondly, though it seems early, you need to get your queen to "ramp up" to those higher levels of eggs laid each day. You really want her to start laying eggs before this time.

Again, consider when this foraging field bee must first appear as an egg. This foraging field bee available to go to work on April 1st is "born" on March 11th (twenty-one days earlier). A worker bee needs 21 days from egg to emergence. Backing up from March 11th by three weeks, you need this egg laid on February 18th.

But the queen doesn't just decide on that one day to lay an egg, nor does she randomly decide to start a family without the proper food available. Honey may be stored from the previous year, but the food of choice for a new generation of larvae is nectar and pollen. Nectar and pollen get the queen excited about laying eggs.

How much nectar and pollen is available on February 18th? Not much, I would guess. But since you want the queen to start laying eggs on the 18th, you have to have pollen and nectar available prior to that date. You need the queen to "ramp up" in her desire to start laying eggs. It might be advantageous for her to start laying a few eggs on February 4th, and in the following two weeks, build up to several hundred eggs, hopefully to a couple thousand by late March and early April.

Tip #1: Stimulative Feeding

To get your queen to think the time is right and stimulate her desire and interest to lay eggs, you almost have to feed your colony a 1:1 syrup as a nectar substitute. A 1:1 ratio is 1 part sugar mixed into 1 part warm water. These "parts" are volume measurement (i.e. cups, scoops, tin cans, whatever).

I feed on the top of the inner cover using plain old, inverted quart jars with a few, very small nail holes punched in the lid. You can also set these inverted jars right over the top bars on top of the brood cluster (if the bees have ascended that high in the hive) or you can make a special inner cover with holes that fit the lids of the jars. Entrance feeders, to me, are worthless if the weather turns cold. You need the feed where the bees are. I only feed on top of the hive with inverted quart jars this early in the spring.

And I'm also not a big fan of those division board feeders, as long as I've brought up the topic of feeding. (These are the feeders that slide into the hive replacing one of the frames). The old style of these feeders was nothing more than huge tanks that drowned the bees. Recently, there have been lots of improvements in these feeders. I still don't like them. Peruse any catalog and you'll see how some have little "ladders" to help the bees get out and reduce the bees that drown.

There are many ways to feed bees. I want a method that delivers the syrup to the bees, even when it's cold and they are less likely to make their way to a remotely placed feeder.

I'm also a big fan of feed additives, though plain 1:1 sugar syrup is very adequate. However, I absolutely LOVE MegaBee and Honey-B-Healthy as two additives to my syrups. You can find these products from any one of the many supply catalogs.

Additionally, if the colony has little or no pollen stored, a pollen substitute is a great idea for a protein source. You can make these or buy them and lay a thin patty of substitute across the top bars. It is my suggestion to put these in place on February 1st (or the first warm day after February 1st), which would set the tone and give the green light for the queen to get into the mood to lay eggs. The main benefit of pollen substitute patties is they feed the young bees that feed the larvae.

I also like to think pollen patties help with winter survival so I'm not opposed to feeding earlier. However, by February 1st, those early patties may be consumed and you need to add more.

If your target date to entice this queen to start laying eggs is still February 18th, a pollen patty on February 1st would give her eighteen days to start laying eggs. Finding a good quality pollen substitute used to be rather difficult and some people suggest that unless real pollen is mixed into the substitute, the bees won't touch it. Now days, all the major suppliers make nutritionally sound pollen supplements that contain real pollen, and they are enhanced with stimulative oils to increase consumption.

It is not unusual for the queen to lay eggs in February anyway, but there won't be many at first. I've had the queen lay eggs in January when the weather has been mild. In many cases, the queen may have already started without your interference or the stimulus of nectar syrup and pollen substitute. Commencing to lay eggs early is a trait of certain races of bees, and other races will hold back until the weather is really settled before they lay their eggs and start to take their foraging responsibilities seriously.

I like to feed the early syrup to give the queen a boost in her egg laying schedule. Some years I get real busy and I don't get out to all my yards when I want to. When I compare the hives given an early feeding of syrup to the "left alone" hives, I see a large difference obviously favoring of the syrup fed hives.

Again, there are many variables, and my observations are fairly anecdotal. But as I encourage my beekeeping buddies to feed early syrup, they come back with the same observations as I do, namely, that feeding an early, light syrup of 1:1 (sugar:water) is beneficial to the hive and accelerates the spring build up.

Tip #2: Overwinter Strong Colonies

Another factor to early egg laying is heat. There must be enough bee bodies present in the hive to keep the brood from being chilled. A strong population of bees left over from the fall will be a great stimulus to egg laying, and younger bees will outlast the older bees going into the winter. The queen will not lay eggs if there are not sufficient bee bodies to cover the larvae and keep them from freezing. This is another reason why you need to overwinter a strong colony.

Do you see how these factors are beginning to work together? You'll continue to see how all five factors will synergize each other, complement each other, balance each other and make your other efforts more effective.

Along these lines of having a warm environment to raise brood is the question about Screen Bottom Boards (SBB). I like to close off my SBB to keep out the drafts. Bear in mind, my hives sit up on elevated hive stands so the risk of winter winds blowing up into the cluster is higher than if my hives sat on pallets. I am one of those guys who likes to close off his screen bottom boards, but other beekeepers will disagree.

I don't think an open SBB helps keep the bees warm in the spring. That's just my opinion. Now in the summer, I'm all for keeping the SBB open as a help for controlling varroa mites. In the fall, I want to close them off when I treat my hives with formic acid. You need to close off the bottom if you're administering formic acid pads, anyway, and I just sleep better during those cold, winter blizzards knowing my SBB are closed off.

A lot of guys tell me they are concerned about ventilation so they want their SBB open during the winter. That's fine, but when it's time to raise brood, I feel like I want them closed. If you have SBB with a slot to slide in a solid board, you're doing well. My SBB are homemade and so I have to go and lift the hive up and slide a piece of board under the hive. It's easier for me to close off my SBB when it's time to administer the formic acid and leave them that way all winter. I don't seem to have any ventilation problems.

In the old days, even with solid bottom boards, you had beekeepers inserting a piece of equipment called the "slatted rack." You don't see these much anymore. They had slats of wood that ran perpendicular to the frames. They were supposed to make the brood nest warmer and entice the queen to start laying eggs earlier.

Since I haven't used slatted racks, I cannot make a recommendation either way. I have, however, left some SBB open during the winters and closed some SBB off (a lot depends on the weather and my work schedule). In the spring, I believe I can tell which ones had the bottoms closed off, and they're the hives that are doing much, much better.

This observation, however, is purely anecdotal. There are a host of variables that go into the spring build up. At one meeting I was sharing this insight, and another beekeeper approached me after the meeting to tell me I was dead wrong.

This other beekeeper said he closed off the SBB on half of his hives, left the other half of his hives open. Guess what? The closed-off hives all died. Therefore, he told me, I was wrong.

Well, there are a host of variables to discern before you go off and say there's only one way to keep bees. I found what works best for me is to close off those SBB in the fall. I have to do it for the formic acid treatment anyway. And I know there are some beekeepers who are just too lazy to close their SBB off so they simply say, "My bees look better when I leave the SBB open all winter long."

Okay. Whatever works for you is what is going to work for you.

Tip #3: Supply Ample Cell Space to Lay Eggs

Another key to this second factor is providing ample room to lay eggs. In the early fall, I will often consolidate the frames in a hive and take out old frames that need culling. I'll also take out empty frames from the bottom of the hive and basically make the hive more compact. This way the bees do not need to heat such a large area. I also want to insure the bees have several frames of honey for them to eat during the winter. Then I can gauge how much syrup the bees need to give them enough for winter survival.

Believe it or not, making the hive configuration smaller in volume makes for better survival. I've had bees survive in a six-frame nuc right next door to a double-brood box hive that died during the winter. And again, there are more variables than I'm aware of, however, it seems to me that smaller volumes make for better survival. But of course, you need to have a sizeable population of bees to keep that area warm, and you need adequate room for feed!

Now here's something I need to remind my beekeeping students. Honey is a winter survival food. Nectar is a springtime brood rearing food. Bees eat honey in the winter to survive, but they will need nectar in the spring to start feeding brood. Bees have been known to collect the humidity from the hive that condenses along the outer walls and dilute honey back to the consistency of nectar. If nectar is not available, the bees will really respond to a little 1:1 syrup provided by the beekeeper.

Okay, so the bees need nectar and not honey. If you prepared your bees for a good winter's rest, you left them ample stores of honey. You should have honey left over when the early spring arrives. But this extra, leftover honey is not really needed. What the bees really need now are empty frames of drawn comb that gives the queen ample space to lay eggs. So what should I do?

In the spring, you will find me taking out extra frames of honey that won't be needed. When I start opening my hives in February or whenever that first real warm spell comes to southeast Missouri, I will take out all the extra frames of honey. I'll rearrange the hive so the two outside frames are honey leaving the inside frames open and empty. I say "empty" but most of my frames still contain quite a bit of pollen and a few thin bands of honey.

I've learned from experience that if too much honey is left in the hive, the queen will not have the room to lay eggs. You can take these frames of honey out and store them for the time when you make nucs. You can extract them and give back the empty frames for the queen to lay eggs. However, if you treated your hives for mites during the fall or fed heavily, do not think about passing off this "honey" as honey for human consumption. If you fed sugar syrup in the fall, this "honey" is probably tainted with sucrose. It can, however, be extracted and diluted 1:1 and fed back to the bees.

So what you'll find me doing at the first nice warm spell in the spring is pulling out all my extra frames of honey, leaving two on the outer walls of the hive, and inserting frames of drawn comb that I stored and protected from the wax moths over the winter. A frame of solid honey is like a brick wall to the bees, and unless they eat it up, it will remain a useless frame as the colony moves into spring.

Now you may be wondering: Okay, you had me feed extra 1:1 syrup as a stimulative feed, but now you're telling me to take out the honey? Why don't I just leave the honey for the bees? Why even feed at all?

Here's a key concept: In the spring the bees do not need honey. I don't know how many times I've preached this concept over and over. Honey is a winter food. In the spring the bees need nectar. They will take honey and dilute it with water they've brought into the hive. Bees have also been known to take the humidity that condenses along the exterior walls and use it to dilute the honey into a consistency of nectar.

But they don't need honey. It's too thick. As a beekeeper, I want to extract it and feed it back after diluting it with water in a ratio of 1 part extracted honey to 1 part warm water.

At this point, I usually get a lecture about the problems of feeding old "honey" back to bees. First, the honey has to be diluted about 1:1 with warm water, and that takes extra work. Second, a big fuss is made to insure this extra honey is from disease-free hives.

Please! If it's from my hives I feel comfortable feeding it back to my own bees. However, if a hive died, the left over honey is going to be robbed out anyway so much of this fuss is just useless fussing.

My point is that left over "honey" (or stored and cured sugar syrup) from your own hives can be diluted and fed back to your own bees. If you leave frames of capped honey in the hive, the bees have to dilute it themselves with water. It is far better to remove the frames of honey, extract them, dilute the honey and feed it back. In the process, you can return those empty extracted frames back to the bees so the queen has more room to lay eggs.

As an alternative, if you're still kind of stuck on taking those frames of honey from the bees is to simply add another brood box with drawn comb. During this warm spell, pull the frames of honey and put it to the outside wall of all of your brood boxes. Place the existing brood frames and the empty drawn comb in the middle of the brood boxes. By adding more frames, you will give the queen more room.

However, I think it's a little early to be giving them more room. Generally, I remove the excess frames of solid honey in February, but I don't add any extra boxes (giving them more room) until after March 20th. (March 20 seems to be a HUGE turning point in our local weather.)

If the queen has ample room to lay eggs, the colony is less likely to swarm. One of the hardships of a rapid spring build up is the potential for swarming. More on that in the next chapter. And again, do you see how these factors are interrelated?

As I've cleared out the extra frames of honey and replaced them with frames of drawn comb, I will need to begin feeding 1:1 syrup, a nectar substitute if natural nectar is not yet available. If my frames are lacking pollen, I will feed a pollen substitute. We've also learned lately that all pollen is not the same, nutritionally speaking. Pollen substitutes are balanced and better for the bees than real pollen. Yes, they cost money and labor to install, but we're looking at investing resources into the hive that pay dividends. A pollen substitute will cost about $2 per hive, and some of the best pollen patties available contain actual pollen.

I know that's a hard concept to wrap your brain around, and until I saw the nutritional analysis of real pollen, I was from the camp that believed anything from nature is better than what humanity can create. And there are those who believe real nectar is better than sugar syrup. Nutritionally and chemically, nectar and 1:1 sucrose syrup are very, very close.

The point is this: give your queen plenty of room to lay and give the bees the nutritional resources to feed the larvae. You do this by pulling out those solid frames of honey and replacing them with frames of drawn comb. If you don't have drawn comb, you can insert frames of wax foundation. Give your queen a reason to start laying eggs early.

Some queens from some races or breeds simply start laying eggs on their own, earlier than what nature dictates. The bees may have sufficient pollen stored from last year. But bear in mind, the queen is very responsible. She will not begin a family of hungry larvae until she knows the colony can provide for them. Don't leave any question in her mind! Give the colony some supplemental feeding and let them know that the time is now to proceed with her egg laying duties.

I highly recommend feeding a pollen substitute anyway. You can spend an extra $2 or $3 per hive on a pollen substitute and a little syrup and call it an insurance policy. It may not help, but it sure won't hurt!

I've made my own pollen substitute that has real pollen in it _and the bees love it_. But as my hive numbers grew, it became easier and less time-consuming to simply buy a commercially prepared patty. The bees love those as well and I buy the ones that have irradiated pollen as one of the ingredients. Irradiated pollen is thought to be disease-free. You can get pollen substitutes with Honey-B-Healthy added in.

I try and feed my pollen patties before the bees are bringing in pollen. My pollen patties are meant to first, stretch the natural supply of incoming pollen, and second, to provide food for those stretches of cool, wet weather that follow those fickle and warm, "teaser" days of sunshine and tree blossoms. My pollen patties are designed to be fed with 1:1 syrup.

I place my pollen patties over the top bars of the brood nest and I feed my syrup form inverted quart jars over a feeding screen, a modified inner cover, or some other method that gets the syrup close to the brood nest. Entrance feeders or "Boardman" feeders don't really work in cold weather.

I've also gotten to the point of placing a pollen patty in the hive in the late fall or early winter when the weather is still fairly mild, relatively speaking. By early spring, it's mostly consumed. Again, it may be viewed as an additional expense, but I see it as good insurance. Added protein will increase the survivability of the bees.

And speaking of good insurance, spring is a good time to feed any of the treatments for nosema, a disease of the bee gut. Nosema is primarily a springtime problem, though a lot of beekeepers treat for it in the fall with their fall syrup feedings. I prefer to treat for it (when I do) in the spring. This disease usually occurs when the hive is damp, humid and cold, and those conditions speak to the weather we have in Missouri.

The key to maximum honey production is series of egg-laying events beginning at least forty-two days prior to the beginning of the honey flow (and it's better if egg laying is happening even earlier!). Then the queen continues with an increasing number of eggs laid with each successive day, which will produce waves of emerging brood who will become the workforce necessary to bring in the nectar that they'll make into honey.

The key to maximizing high honey yields is to have this workforce ready to go as the blooms come forth with their nectar. To get the workforce ready, you need to feed pollen substitute and 1:1 sugar syrup to entice the queen into laying those early eggs. Bear in mind you need a good, prolific queen, and you need a good strong population of young bees going into the winter. In the spring, clear out the brood nest of all that extra honey that won't be consumed anyway. Make sure you have a good population of bees to keep the brood warm.

But now we have qualified a second necessary step in making this second factor a reality: you need a good queen.

Both her age and her genetic or racial make-up will be a factor. Races vary in their desire to lay early brood. It is generally believed that Italians will start laying earlier (and also later in the fall) but they are notorious hogs when it comes to eating up your winter stores. Russians tend to shut down egg laying in the fall sooner, and they're slower to start laying eggs in the spring. They are, however, very frugal and over winter well in a tiny cluster. While they have a resistance to mites, they don't seem to bring in ample supplies of nectar and convert it into honey.

And I also clarify something else. When you order queens, the producer will ask you about the race or variety you want. I am under the opinion, especially with open-mated queens, that there are no longer any "pure" breeds of bees. We are blending and homogenizing the races based on behavioral selection (i.e. hygienic behavior) rather than genetic purity.

And this is not a bad thing.

I am, more and more, switching to annual requeening. It used to be the common consensus was to requeen every other year. I want young, summer queens to lead my hives into the winter. Young queens lay more eggs going into the fall and they seem to lay eggs earlier in the spring.

I also used to order queens in the spring, then fight the competition as everyone else wanted queens in the spring. Once they arrived, I had to fight the fickle spring weather.

Then I started thinking about how those mail-order queens need five to seven days to get accepted before they come out of their mailing cage. Then I had some bad queens, likely poorly mated during cold spring weather. Then the colony set about superseding that queen. Some of my queens were killed and the colony went queenless.

All of these factors leave a gap in time when I don't have any eggs laid, which contributed to a gap in the work force.

And mail-order queens kept getting more expensive. Shipping got more expensive. Then the post office got stingy on insuring live deliveries.

So I started thinking about raising my own queens in the summer, then requeening my hives in August, along with splitting my big hives into smaller nucs or "singles." I could get my own queens settled in my nucs and splits, test them out, evaluate them, insure they were accepted, then bring that hive through the winter into spring.

What I found is that an overwintered colony with an established queen less than one year of age becomes a dynamite egg-laying machine. I also found that queens that emerged after the "change of days"

(June 22) tend to lay more eggs into the fall than their older counterparts.

I am fully convinced raising one's own summer queens to make one's own splits in late summer/early fall is the way to go. Some people raise queens because they think it's cheaper. I'm not so sure it is. You do, however, have to put in a lot of work to raise those queens and it might be a trade-off between the cost of new mail-order queens and the time it takes to raise my own.

I will contend you get better control over the quality of the queens when you raise your own. Imagine raising a hundred queens and you get to keep only the top producers as you evaluate the queens going into winter. You don't subject your own queens to the shipping and introductory stress (and possible rejection) and you don't have to fight the fickle spring weather to get them introduced.

More and more, I am convinced to requeen all my hives in the summer (basically making splits to introduce my newly raised queens) and only keep one-year old queens.

However, I still keep many of the best queens around for another year. They become my breeding stock, my source of eggs for next year's queen crop. But more and more, I'm getting used to the idea of requeening and making splits in the summer after the honey flow is over.

Young queens are the best way to maximizing your honey production. Young queens are more prolific and reduce the swarming impulse. Raising your own queens that flourish under your management and are locally adapted to your area are better yet than anything you'll get through the mail.

I've also learned that a good young queen raised under optimum conditions and well-mated is superior to a genetically selected queen raised under stressful conditions. Summer offers the best mating weather, as well as sufficient nectar and pollen to give the queen larvae the best nutrition.

Tip #4: Intersperse Open Frames into the Broodnest

One of the things you will notice is how the broodnest becomes rather compact. The bees keep the brood nest compact to retain heat and to keep the larvae warm and incubated.

If you add another brood box, or if you reverse the brood boxes, you will notice how the bees tend to move up, vertically, rather than out, horizontally. You'll find brood in the middle four frames in each box, leaving the outer frames vacant. Or you'll find the bees will move up on one side of the box as opposed to the center. When bees move up we call this behavior as "chimneying," like moving up in a vertical direction like they were creating a narrow chimney.

One of the tricks given to me by several older beekeepers is to pull one of the empty frames from outside the brood nest. Create a vacancy in the middle of the brood nest by sliding several frames over toward the side where the empty frame was previously located. Now insert the empty frame into the vacancy in the middle of the brood nest.

Obviously you have to have empty frames to do this. If you still have ample stores of honey from the winter, you can pull out one frame of solid honey from outside the brood nest, slide the frames over, then bring in a frame of drawn comb from your winter storage.

This manipulation will invite the bees to prepare the empty frame for the queen. The heat from the middle of the brood nest will encourage her to lay eggs in these cells. Then as this frame is filled up and bees are emerging from the cells on other frames, you can pull another frame from the outside, create another vacancy in the middle of the brood nest by sliding the frames over to the side, and then inserting the empty frame into the middle of the brood nest.

This method is also explained in the next chapter on swarm prevention as it works to prevent congestion. It's aggressive, and some people fear it will cause the brood to get "chilled." If the hive is robust and healthy, with lots of bees to cover the brood and keep it warm, there is little danger of chilling the brood. Further, if you do it gradually, one frame at a time, the potential of chilling is small.

This method is also called "checkerboarding" when you do it to two or more boxes of brood. It's a neat little trick to intersperse empty frames into the middle of the brood nest to accelerate the queen's ability and availability to lay eggs. This trick also entices the bees to draw out frames of bare foundation faster than if the frames were left to the outer perimeter of the brood nest.

It seems the location of the brood rearing retains most of the young bees that still have active wax glands. The heat from the brood nest makes this an ideal location for making and molding the wax scales into drawn comb. This will hasten foundation being drawn into comb.

Tip #5: Choosing Races That Naturally Build Up Rapidly

The next step is to select a breed of honeybee that has rapid spring build up and good nectar gathering habits. The two breeds I favor are Italians and Carniolans, and lately I've added the Buckfast to my line-up. The various strains and breeding lines within these breeds differ in their quality, so it's hard to give solid recommendation that any one breed is the key to maximum honey production. Many breeders concede there are no "pure" breeds of bees anymore. We've blended the lines and hybridized the characteristics.

Further, even great honey producing breeds won't do any good if they are highly susceptible to disease or mites. At the present time, some of the larger pollinators are bringing in imported Australian honeybees (Australia's season ends about the time ours is picking up in February). However, as they have shown themselves to be good honey producers, these bees from "down under" have a higher susceptibility to varroa mites.

So pick your races of bees with your needs in mind. Interestingly, most beekeepers select breeds of honeybees known for their gentleness. Gentleness is not necessarily the antithesis of honey production, but it seems mean bees produce more honey. I have some hives that produce a ton of honey, but their disposition is that of a grizzly bear. If they didn't produce so well, I'd select a different breed.

I've even purchased some supposedly "gentle" bees from southern queen producers that advertised "gentle" bees. They showed pictures in their advertisements of their workers opening hives with no protection. But when I ordered, I didn't get those gentle bees. When I ordered from these producers I got the aggressive cousins instead! But they were good honey producers and that is my number one criteria for keeping a particular strain of honeybee.

However, as you select replacement queens from reputable queen breeders, patronize those breeders who provide you with superior stock. Don't feel that you have to produce your own queens yourself. I find it's more convenient for me to wait until summer and raise my own queens, but I'm always buying some new queens each year to diversify my genetic base.

Obviously, you need to know which strains of which breeds from which particular queen breeder is the one for you and your area. This knowledge is something you need to determine at least a year in advance. It's for this reason that I'll keep a good queen around for a second year. She'll become my breeding stock to raise new queens from.

Along with a good spring build-up through early egg laying, I've found some strains of bees get out earlier to forage. I've walked through my bee yards just as the sun began to dip below the horizon. Some of my hives are still working at dusk while some hives have called it quits. I also notice how some hives work better under the cloudy and cool weather. These are my "go-getter" bees.

I watch these hives and consider the possibility of raising new queens from this stock. Rapid spring build up is one thing, foraging under less-than-ideal situations is another factor I like. I also like to raise my own queens from several different breeder queens to continue to mix up my genes.

I'm also a more natural kind of beekeeper. I don't use any of the hard chemicals and miticides. I favor Integrated Pest Management and the "soft" chemicals and treatments. I also need a bee that can survive and tolerate a certain level of mites. When I buy breeding stock, I keep an eye out for those producers that sell queens with known "hygienic" behavior.

And let me again repeat myself when it comes to clearing out that old honey (or stored sugar syrup from your ample fall feedings). I've heard complaints from my beekeeping buddies about how that good old queen from last year just "played out" over the winter and won't lay any eggs in the spring. They ask me to come by for a visit to inspect their hives. And they're dead-set on buying a new queen to replace that old, failing queen.

But when we open their hives on a warm day, I find the brood nest absolutely clogged with wall to wall honey. The open areas, what little are present, are filled with brood, but there just are not too many of these. Those good old queens didn't "play out," but rather they couldn't lay eggs even if they wanted to (and most want to!). You can do all the other things that lead to quality queens, but if you don't clear out the brood nest, leaving a maximum of two frames of leftover honey, you won't reach your maximum potential for that hive. So let me repeat myself:

The third step in creating a mighty foraging work force is creating an open brood nest for the queen to lay eggs. It does no good to feed pollen substitute and 1:1 syrup to a hive headed with a young queen if she has no place to lay eggs. Too many hives have more than enough frames of left-over honey and pollen from the previous season.

This is always a good thing when you make sure the colony has ample reserves for their winter survival, but come spring, this good thing will become a limitation to the queen. In the spring, you need to do some spring cleaning and clear out the left over honey.

In that first part of February, or when the days provide me with the warmth to open the hive and slip in a pollen patty, I will sort through the frames and pull out the extra, solid frames of honey. In a ten frame brood box, I want the two outer frames to be honey and the inside frames to be a mix of honey, some pollen and mostly open cells for the queen to lay eggs. This may mean I need to have frames of drawn comb in storage, protected from wax moths.

If I have to, I will remove frames of honey and extract them, or even replace the frames with bare foundation. Given the right stimulus (1:1 syrup) the bees will draw it out, but it also takes a pretty strong hive with lots of workers to generate enough heat to warm the hive and draw out foundation in February.

If the honey was treated with miticides going into the winter, you cannot extract it for human consumption in the spring. I suggest extracting the honey, then cutting the honey with equal parts of water and feeding it back to the bees.

I've also seen hives where the frames were simply clogged with way too much pollen that the queen had no place to lay. If she cannot lay eggs, then the whole point of the other factors is moot. Remove the frames clogged with pollen and give fresh frames of foundation if you do not have drawn comb.

If the colony is strong and can generate enough heat for a warm environment, they will draw out wax if fed an ample supply of nectar substitute (1:1 syrup). It is better to have them drawing out wax than having the queen sitting around doing nothing because all the frames are full of honey.

Maximum honey production is attained by having a mighty force of age-appropriate foragers in place prior to the honey flow. For this to happen you need to stimulate a queen to lay eggs early by feeding 1:1 syrup and pollen patties. You need a young, mated queen in place, ready to go with lots of empty space to lay eggs.

This means you need to get into your hives as early as you can and get to work. Any day when the temperatures reach 60 degrees is a day you need to be opening your hives and making sure things are right for a rapid spring build up.

And of course, you need good weather to manipulate the hive to make all this possible. Even the best laid plans of mice, men and beekeepers go awry because of weather and work commitments and family obligations. The bees will always do what comes naturally to them, but it is the beekeeper who holds the power within his or her hands to make the conditions right to maximize their potential.

This is the second factor in managing your hives for maximum production. But with rapid spring build up comes the potential for triggering the swarm impulse. That's the next chapter.

Addendum to Chapter 5

Frame Management

Let me intersperse a short chapter on frame management, or better yet, "comb" management.

In most managerial schemes in beekeeping, you're going to have two kinds of drawn comb. There is the first kind of comb in the brood-rearing area, and the second kind of comb that the bees will use primarily for ripening nectar into honey. The brood comb will quickly become dark and strong, the honey comb will mostly retain its light color.

Now as I practice an open brood nest, I allow my queen to move up into the area that will eventually become my honey supers destined for extraction. Obviously I have to wait until the brood matures and emerges before that comb can be extracted. And yes, the presence of brood will darken my honey. But as the summer progresses, the queen moves down and the upper boxes are filled with honey.

So basically I have two kinds of comb in my beehive: the older, darker brood comb and the "mostly lighter" comb from the honey supers. By the way, did you know where that name, "super" comes from? It comes from the old days when beekeepers kept their bees in double brood boxes. They never manipulated the frames or bothered looking for the queen. The colony was pretty much left as is, undisturbed.

When the honey flow started, they would add the smaller honey "supers" on top of the brood boxes. These smaller boxes were "superimposed" on top of the brood nest. Then they were removed for extraction or the production of comb honey. The lower boxes were left as they were. Hence the shortened name, "supers" for being "superimposed" upon the brood nest.

We know more information about honeybee biology these days. We know more information about diseases and pest as well. It's interesting how our basic ideals of lower brood boxes and upper honey supers hasn't changed.

But back to my original thought: You're going to have two kinds of boxes with frames that are used for different purposes. You have your brood frames and your honey frames. Many beekeepers will use queen excluders (a screened, wire grid that keeps the queen out of the honey supers) to keep the two kinds of boxes separate.

In my operation, using the "open brood nest," it's not uncommon to have brood hatch out in my honey supers. But basically, there are two kinds of hive bodies and two kinds of purposes.

Let's start with the honey frames. These frames are removed for extraction and stored for the winter. I highly recommend protecting these frames from wax moths if wax moths are a problem in your area. The most common fumigant is paradichlorobenzene, or PDB, sold under the name "para-moth." Follow the instructions and your frames will be safe.

Further, wax moths prefer brood comb, but don't think that preference is going to keep your honey frames safe from wax moths. You still need to take the measures to protect your honey supers from wax moths, even if your honey frames are used solely for honey. I can't say it enough: protect your drawn honey super comb.

Why? Because I've watched my bees during an intense nectar flow. When the nectar flow is coming on like gang-busters (ever wonder what a gang-buster is?), the bees need to put that nectar some place in the hive. If there is no comb drawn out in the upper boxes or honey supers, their first resort is to put that nectar in the brood nest.

If there is a nectar flow going on, it's also likely the queen is laying eggs like crazy. Now the brood nest is being filled with nectar and the queen wants the space for egg laying. This activity will trigger swarming if the brood nest is congested with nectar and brood.

Eventually, the bees will start to draw out the wax foundation you give them and store the nectar, but it's best to have that comb already drawn out. I cannot preach this enough: protect your drawn comb! When you give it to the bees, the colony will need it to store nectar. I'll hit this point again when I talk about supering your bees.

So my first point is to protect your drawn comb in your honey supers. Do not let the wax moths eat it up and make the bees do all that work over! Protect them and keep them for the next year.

Now my second point will sound contradictory: replace the drawn comb in the brood nest.

WHAT?

You just said to do everything possible to protect and preserve the drawn comb in the honey super and now you're telling me to pull and replace the drawn comb in the brood nest. What gives?

These frames in the brood nest have a different purpose. You'll see them darken the more they are used. They collect old larval moltings, pupal skins, fecal matter from the larvae. That's enough for me to replace them.

But these are also the frames that are on your hives when you treat for mites. If you use the approved chemical miticides, it may surprise you to know that these brood frames accumulate and retain some of that chemical. Over time, they accumulate a lot of that chemical. It gets to the point that these "safe" chemicals are now building to lethal (i.e. unsafe) levels. Being on the hive year-round also brings in a host of environmental pollutants.

It is now recommended that beekeepers pull out and replace 20% of their frames, which means every year you pull out 2 out of every ten frames. Yes, this sounds expensive, but today you can buy a wood frame for about $1 and the wax for about $1.20 per sheet. I'm asking you to invest about $2.50 each year into your hive to help promote the health of the hive. Fresh frames of new wax give the queen a nicer place to lay eggs and the bees are healthier. Healthier bees build up faster and bring in more nectar.

And if you wish, you can tear out or boil out the old wax and reuse the wood frame. But having been there and done that, it is better to burn the old black comb and start from scratch. Time is money and it takes a lot of time to tear out or boil those old frames.

But there's another small problem. The sheets of wax foundation you buy from the supply companies have been tested. Would it surprise you to know that they've found residues of chemical miticides in those sheets of wax foundation? That wax, of course, came from beekeepers who sold their wax to the supply companies after they used it in their hives treated with chemical miticides.

So what I've done is I've bought wood frames and I wire them as if I'm going to slip in a sheet of wax foundation. Instead, I glue popsicle sticks in the wedge bar groove to give the bees a guide to draw out their own foundation. When you take these frames (now called foundationless frames) with popsicle sticks in place of wax foundation, and you place it in the brood nest between two existing frames of drawn comb, the bees will draw that foundationless frame just as straight as an arrow. This also means my cost per frame was cut in half.

So just a timely tip about managing your frames and comb. Plan on protecting your honey supers, but plan on replacing 20% of your brood frames each year. In both cases, though it sounds contradictory, you'll be better off.

The key concept of protecting honey supers is to accelerate the rate of nectar storage. The key concept of replacing brood frames is to replace old, diseased/polluted frames with clean comb for the queen to lay eggs.

Chapter 6: Swarm Prevention

The Third Factor

If everything has gone well so far, you've brought a strong population of bees through the winter. They're healthy, and the large population of bees has started the spring build up and you're off to a nice start. Last fall you requeened with a young queen and treated for mites. You provided ample syrup to insure good stores for winter.

Now in the spring, you've cleared the brood nest of all that old honey and replaced those frames with empty comb for maximum egg laying opportunities. Now you have a new generation of young bees getting ready to go out and forage with a vengeance. You have the space to store all that dilute nectar. You're set!

But watch out! If you don't prevent swarming, then all your hard work is going to leave and start a new colony somewhere else, somewhere else where you won't be able to harvest their honey.

The third factor in maximum honey yields is preventing the bees' natural impulse to swarm. And unfortunately, the "penalty" for doing everything right and getting your bees off to a prosperous start is swarming.

The swarming impulse is totally natural. The bees are wired to divide the colony during abundant times and set up a new (or several) new hives in the neighborhood. Bees naturally want to swarm in order to perpetuate the species in that given area. It multiplies the colonies in the event some of the colonies die out or their home is destroyed.

And when the circumstances are favorable (like when you do everything right) the opportunities to swarm are much, much higher. Unfortunately, the consequences are more costly as well.

Think of a factory that manufactures widgets. Life is good, the supplies are delivered, the staff is content, sales are going good. But the foreman in charge decides to take half of the workforce and start a competing business in a vacant warehouse across town.

So what happens to the factory? Well, for starters, they have no leader. So they have to draft a foreman from the ranks of the workers. Half of the workers have left so production is cut in half. You have idle machinery because you don't have the personnel to run it. It takes time to advertise, interview and hire new employees.

Now this factory will survive, but its economic production is set back. The old foreman who left is busy setting up his shop so there's not much hope he'll have much production for a few months.

And it's possible for both factories to succeed, but with the departure of the foreman and half the work force, the productivity of the factory is horribly disrupted. It will take time for the new factory to fire up and become productive, but remember the rationale for splitting the factory was a very favorable economic environment.

And so it is with swarming. When the environment is favorable with good weather, ample nectar and pollen, the old queen leaves and starts a new hive with half of the work force. It's horribly disruptive to the original hive, but both will likely survive...but it has costs. Those costs are honey production.

I hate swarming. I despise swarming. I feel chagrined and stupid when my bees swarm on me. When I see a swarm leave one of my hives or when I see a bundle of bees clustered high on a branch, all I can see is about sixty to ninety pounds of honey flying away.

It's maddening, but I have to remind myself it's natural. It's part of their instinct. And when the situation and circumstances are favorable, the bees are much, much more likely to swarm. But if you are after monster honey yields or if you're managing your hives for maximum honey production, then swarming is something you will need to prevent. And because you're creating an ideal, exceptionally favorable environment, the swarming impulse will be easily triggered.

So how do you prevent something that is naturally wired into the brains of all those bees? I think the answer is easy: You have to redirect their energies so they think about something else. And quite frankly, volumes of literature have been written on varieties swarm techniques. Let me give you some general advice on the subject.

We speak a lot of swarm prevention or swarm control. But I've found the best way to keep your hives from swarming is to redirect their energies and rewrite their agenda. Keep them busy. Give them ample room. Provide ample frames of drawn comb for the queen to lay eggs.

Super early so the foragers have a place to store incoming nectar. Don't let them even start to think they're going to need to swarm. And like everything else in keeping honeybees, all this has to be done BEFORE the conditions tell the bees it's time to swarm.

Understanding Swarming:

If you don't yet understand swarming, it is part of the colony's agenda. Every spring, when the nectar starts to flow and the queen is laying eggs like crazy, and if more room is not provided, the hive will become congested. Congestion triggers swarming.

I use that term "congested" to mean the available cell space on each frame is reduced. The queen is laying more and more eggs. The field bees are bringing in more and more nectar. Pretty soon, the spaces on each frame run short. All the cells are being tied up with dilute nectar and pupating larvae.

The queen is waiting for a pupated worker bee to emerge so she can lay another egg. But the field bees, bringing in more nectar, are looking for that same vacant cell to place their load of nectar. It's like a traffic jam when everybody is trying to use the same roads every morning at eight o'clock when they're rushing to get their children to school and themselves to work. The roadway can't handle the load and something has to give.

When this congestion in the hive happens, something has to give. That's when the workers pick seven to fifteen larvae and feed them copious amounts of royal jelly to convert them into queen cells.

Once the queen cells are capped and begin their pupal stage, the old queen leaves with half of the colony's work force. It is unknown how the colony divides itself on who leaves with the old queen and who stays to welcome the new queen. It just happens.

So the old queen leaves with half of the work force in what we call the "prime" swarm. They go out and search for a hollow tree or some other cavity in which to start a new home. The old queen flies out and lands on a nearby branch. The swarming workers follow. They will cluster on that branch while the older worker bees (those foragers who are familiar with the territory) seek out a suitable location to start the new colony. More than likely, this new location is the cavity in a hollow tree.

Once the new location is found, the swarm cluster breaks up and the bees fly off in a disperse cloud to the new location. Wax is immediately drawn out and the queen starts laying eggs as soon as she can. A new colony is formed and the species continues to thrive.

So Why Is Swarming So Bad?

Now before the old queen leaves with the prime swarm, she has to go on a diet. The bees quit feeding her to make her light enough to fly. She also stops laying eggs. Right way you should recognize that the population of the hive will be diminished because she stops laying eggs.

Once she leaves with the swarm, there will be several days to a week before the new queen emerges, then several more days while she matures, mates and settles down to lay any eggs. The colony might go two weeks without any new eggs being laid. Given the fact that it takes three weeks to grow from an egg to an emerged worker bee, you now have five weeks before a new generation starts taking care of the hive.

Now you've lost half of your work force with the swarm, and you now have a gap in which no eggs are laid that leads to a diminished population which will lead to a gap in the work force, which will, in turn, diminish the nectar coming into the colony. A colony that swarms will not live up to its potential, and in most years, you will be lucky to get any harvestable honey. Some years you're lucky if they survive the next winter.

This is why I don't like my hives to swarm!

Further, to add insult to injury, the colony may raise multiple queens. After the old queen leaves, the queen cells start to hatch. The first new queen out of her cell, after a day or two of maturing, will fly off with half of the existing work force left behind from the prime swarm. We call these "after" swarms as they come after the prime swarm. This first queen will leave with half of the half that was left behind.

The next queen to emerge will leave with half of the half of the half that was left behind. The next queen will leave with her half of the half of the half of the half that was left behind.

You get the picture? The colony grows smaller and smaller.

This is why I am passionate about preventing swarming. Do everything you can to prevent swarming. When your colony swarms, you basically give away your honey crop, then if the colony swarms multiple times, you endanger its survivability.

There are two levels to this subject of swarming. The first, and ideal, is swarm prevention. The second, less desirable, is swarm control. The third, if it gets to this point, is swarm management.

We won't discuss swarm management because it means your hive has swarmed and you find that cluster hanging on a branch, or worse, it got away from you. Now you have a damaged colony with a diminished future. That's another one of my books and let's hope that when you get called to capture a swarm, it's from someone else's hive and not one of yours.

If you're interested, visit:

www.createspace.com/4107714 and

www.createspace.com/4106626.

So let's look at the two real options, swarm prevention and swarm control.

Swarm Control:

Swarming is a natural instinct of the honeybee, and thus your efforts to retard or even eliminate an issue of a swarm is a challenge to your management skills. It takes work to prevent swarming.

However, just as swarming is the result of several factors and conditions, you can likewise apply several management techniques to address those factors and conditions, and hopefully reduce your chances of swarming. The great irony is that if you have done everything right and have a healthy, robust hive of honeybees, you are more likely to have them swarm. What an irony to reward sound management with a swarm!

Some beekeepers seem to think swarming is "no big deal." I beg to differ. Or technically, I would agree: it is true it is not just "a big deal," it is a **HUGE** deal. I would rather admit I had to take my cousin to the high school prom than confess my colonies swarmed. If you don't prevent swarming, you're just giving away your honey crop.

And because my major goal and purpose in keeping honeybees is to produce the maximum crop of honey, swarming is antithetical to my goal and purpose. Now if harvesting handsome crops of honey is not your purpose, then don't worry about it. If you don't care if you get any honey this year, you have nothing to fret: Let your bees swarm all they want.

In the last section, I noted you need a vibrant, productive queen to give you lots of workers. Lots of workers will bring in lots of nectar. With the addition of more incoming nectar, the queen starts laying more eggs. However, high populations of brooding larvae create congestion in the brood chamber. Congestion leads to swarming. Congestion is the competition of nectar and larvae in the brood chamber, and the lack of space for the queen to lay more eggs while more nectar is coming in from the foraging workers.

In my first year of beekeeping, I ordered nucs. I set the nucs up in ten-frame brood boxes and gave them plastic foundation to fill out the remaining frames. I fed them about a gallon of sugar syrup. Then, without warning, my bees started swarming. Some old timers suggested the plastic foundation caused the bees to swarm. I thought so, too.

But my bees were somewhat reluctant to draw out the plastic foundation. They continued to work with the frames of drawn comb that came with the nuc. While ignoring the new, plastic foundation, they filled up the five frames with brood and incoming nectar and the sugar syrup I provided. It wasn't long before they had no more room (cell space) for any more eggs and no storage space for the incoming nectar.

I reached the state of congestion and all at once, they started swarming on me. I quickly nailed together some more boxes, put them on the hives hoping add more space would stop the rest of my hives from swarming.

Nope. They swarmed, too. When I opened the hives, I found some of the most beautiful frames of wall-to-wall brood from the young, productive queens that came with my nucs. But no room for anymore nectar. Congestion triggered the swarm impulse.

"Congestion" is not the same as "crowding" which is the number of bees per square inch. Some guys will open a hive and see a nice cluster of adult worker bees and exclaim, "You better do something about that crowded hive or they will swarm on you."

You can have lots of bees and still have plenty of room (cell space) to store nectar and lay eggs. The key is to provide the bees with ample cell space to store nectar and give the queens lots of space in which to lay eggs. It really is that simple. Unfortunately, we don't think the bees are ready to swarm, or we get busy, or we haven't ordered the extra equipment we need.

The excuses go on forever.

I can't help but emphasize the fact that the congestion that triggers swarming often happens weeks before the bees actually swarm. I've looked at hives I thought had plenty of cell space. Then we got an influx of warm weather which pushed the flowers to produce nectar and the warm weather kicked the queen into laying more eggs.

Just when you thought you had it all figured out. The goal of swarm prevention is to keep plenty of drawn comb **ahead** of the need. Of if you are working with foundation, keep adding new foundation (typically set between frames of existing brood) for the bees to work on. Stay ahead of the curve!

The bottom line is you have to prevent swarming to capture the monster crop of honey. This is where I lose a lot of potential beekeepers who want to manage their hives for maximum production. They get discouraged because they worked so hard to produce a healthy, robust hive only to lose the productivity to swarming.

But it's just not that hard to prevent swarming. But you just have to be ahead of the game and be proactive. You have to provide the bees with more frames of open comb to accommodate a growing population of bees and an increasing influx of nectar.

The third factor for maximum honey production is swarm prevention, an attendant problem that comes with a huge population of worker bees and a congested brood box. When you do everything right, you write a recipe that encourages swarming. So how do you go about preventing swarming?

Tip #1: Requeen with Young Queens:

One way to minimize swarming is to use a young queen. A young queen has more queen "substance," which is a pheromone "glue" that holds the hive population together. When the queen is born, she has her highest levels of the queen substance, and with each day it diminishes.

The greater the queen substance, the less likely the colony is to swarm. Old queens head colonies that are more prone to swarming because their levels of this pheromone drop to levels that cause dissatisfaction and disunity. My young queen from the fall is one factor to reduce their inclination to swarm in the spring.

However, even when you have extraordinarily high populations of workers, this pheromone does not get distributed to all the workers, thus it seems the queen is becoming ineffective. The dissipation of the queen's pheromone will trigger the impulse to swarm. The best, simplest advice is to keep young queens in your colonies. But this is only one part of the solution.

Tip #2: Make Splits:

A second method of alleviating these conditions is to split the colonies. Splitting is simple and very effective. In the most basic of terms, you take one colony and split it into two colonies. The traditional method is to buy a mail-order queen in the early spring and introduce it to the split that has no queen. You then give each split (the original colony with the old queen and the new colony with the new queen) ample boxes and manage them for ample room for brood expansion and nectar storage.

Making splits in the spring is very effective, easy and wide-spread in the beekeeping industry. There are many different ways to make splits and there's a ton of information out there on which method may work best for you.

Personally, I don't care for this method. It will, however, stop the colony from swarming. But since I've had issues with mail-order queens, I prefer to do something else.

However, splitting is a great method of redirecting the colony's energy into something productive and constructive. What I have come to realize is that two smaller colonies (the original and the split) will, together, make a decent honey crop. But it will not be as great as if you left the original hive intact and provided other methods of reducing the swarms.

I'm not against splitting as a means to prevent swarming. It works for a lot of beekeepers. It also increases the number of your hives. But as I said earlier, I have issues with mail-order, southern-produced queens. I hate fighting the bad weather in the early spring. And I think it's better to make my splits in the late summer or fall.

Another downside to making splits is that it means you need to have multiple locations for more hives and you need more equipment. I know several beekeepers who have twenty-five hives and they don't want any more. When they make a split, they sell the split as a five-frame nuc. And they still don't get the honey crop they would have had if they did something else to prevent swarming!

Tip #3: Make a Vertical Split:

There is a method of making a split if you still want to avoid a swarming incident, and you don't need a mail-order queen. It's often called a "Demaree" manipulation. It's very effective. It's also very old.

Let's say you have your bees in two brood-sized boxes. By the early spring they are mostly in the top box and you go in and take out all the extra frames of solid honey and give the queen new frames of drawn comb. She fills these up. Nectar is coming in nicely. You need to give here more room.

The Demaree manipulation has you move the queen to the bottom box. Give her two or three, maybe four frames of brood and bees, maybe a frame of pollen and honey and fill the rest of this box with empty drawn comb. On top of this bottom box, set a new, empty brood box with ten frames of drawn comb (foundation will also work). On top of this empty box, set the top box from the original configuration with the remaining brood and bees.

What you end up with, starting at the bottom is one brood box with the queen and a few frames of bees and brood. Here she will continue to lay eggs. As she continues to lay eggs, she will eventually begin to move upward into the empty brood box. The brood nest will continue to expand unimpeded. This is a good thing. By adding the empty box over the queen you have reduced the likelihood of congestion.

But what about that third box (the old top box) that was filled with the remaining bees and brood? By the time the queen moves up into this top box, the pupated workers will have emerged, the cell space will be available. You've given the queen more space to lay more eggs and you've continued your second factor of promoting a rapid spring build up. Then, if you wish, you can reverse the boxes placing the bottom box on top and the queen will keep laying.

This Demaree manipulation has one drawback in that the upper box may not sense the presence of the queen all the way down in the bottom box. But don't worry about it. They may begin to raise their own queen. I let the colony sort out which queen they want to follow. It really is the case where nature has to take over.

By the time the queen has moved up to the top, I like to reverse my boxes. Now it's generally time to add honey supers. Once the nectar starts flowing in earnest, the bees redirect their energies away from swarming and back to producing honey.

If there was a downside to this method of swarm prevention, you end up with some really tall hives with all the supers stacked on top of them (and one way to alleviate the height of the hives is the fifth factor to managing your hives for maximum production: harvest early, harvest often). Tall hives mean supers are harder to reach and harder to remove when filled with capped honey. And when I've described this system, the biggest complaint I've heard from other beekeepers is how they don't want to have three brood boxes. And if the bees store nectar in those brood boxes, they don't want to harvest it. Those boxes are heavy.

There are a lot of good ways to keep bees, and someone is going to come up with an excuse every time.

Tip #4: Reverse the boxes:

Reversing the brood boxes is like a Demaree manipulation. The nice thing about reversing brood boxes is that you don't need to have a third brood box. This is an easy method for those who don't have extra equipment or don't have the luxury of having extra room for more hives.

To reverse your brood boxes means you switch the top box for the bottom box. And once the top box (the old bottom box) is full of bees and brood, you reverse them again. After the reversal, the queen moves to the lower box, she then works her way up to the upper box. The boxes are reversed and she's back down below. What makes this reversal special is the queen thinks she's working upward when in fact she's just covering old ground.

This method of swarm prevention is very effective, but to reverse the hive bodies, this means you need to have your colony in a minimum of two standard brood boxes or at least three Illinois (medium) supers. The queen prefers to work her way up. When the upper brood box becomes loaded with eggs and larvae (mostly concentrated on the middle frames), the queen will slow down her egg laying rate.

If you reverse the brood boxes (placing the empty bottom box on top of the top box), the queen has fresh frames to lay her eggs as she moves up. Watch her as she will concentrate her egg laying on the middle frames.

But be careful. If you switch brood boxes too often in the early part of the spring, the brood becomes divided between the two boxes. The workers may not be able to keep the brood on two levels warm enough for survival if the weather turns severely cold (another reason I like to close off my SBB).

A suggested time table to reverse your boxes is every ten days, but a prudent beekeeper inspects the hives to see of this is truly timely. You need to start checking your boxes in February if the weather cooperates.

On warm days (over 60 degrees) open the hive and check on the cluster. The queen doesn't like to move down, but allow her the time to spread out. If you see brood on six of your ten frames, it's time to reverse. Don't wait for the queen to fill the outer two frames. It's not likely she will, particularly if the weather is cold, but then again, sometimes she won't follow my advice and you'll find wall-to-wall brood!

I suggest a schedule of every ten days to reverse your brood boxes. But early in the season, the queen may not be laying at a rate fast enough to justify a reversal after ten days. Later in May, ten days may be just right for reversing. Don't guess. Inspect your bees.

If there is no need to reverse, or if you feel it is not quite time, you may want to bring in an empty frame from the edge of the brood nest as I suggested in Tip #4 from chapter 4. This gives the queen a fresh frame in the middle of the brood zone to fill where it is warm, but if the weather turns really cold, the frames you moved closer to the outside may get too cold and the brood will die, but it's got to get really cold and you really have to stretch out the brood nest for this to be a grave concern.

If you find a great brood explosion, you may need to add another brood box or super just for the brood. The point of reversing, checkerboarding and even the Demaree method is to stay ahead of the queen's desire to lay eggs and the incoming rush of nectar that causes congestion and triggers swarming. The key words are "STAY AHEAD." Swarm prevention is a proactive management skill.

Keep reversing brood boxes as you find the queen moving up. Also, if you reverse the boxes and your pollen substitute patty is on the top box (which is now on the bottom) you will benefit by adding another patty on top of the frames in the new upper brood chamber. The bees need the food where the eggs are laid and the larvae develop.

Tip #5: Checkerboarding:

Checkerboarding is my favorite method of swarm prevention. It's like a Demaree manipulation with the simplicity of reversing the brood boxes. Like the Demaree manipulations, it's an older tradition sometimes referred to as the "Open Brood Nest."

In a nutshell, you open the hive on a warm, sunny day when most of the field bees are out foraging. Bring with you another brood box and empty frames of drawn comb. Tear apart the hive and basically redistribute the frames from two brood boxes into three brood boxes.

Separate frames of brood with empty frames of drawn comb. Restack the brood boxes and in essence, create a "checkerboarded" pattern of alternating frames of brood and empty comb side to side and top to bottom.

Basically, you alternate frames of brood with empty frames. If can imagine how a checkerboard looks with alternating black and red squares, that's how the beehive will be arranged as you look at it from the front. In its purest sense, the frames will alternate from side to side (left to right) and top to bottom (from one brood box to the next).

Don't let this method sound too complicated. It's not rocket science. I think of it as stretching out the brood nest from side to side and top to bottom, simply interspersing empty frames between frames of brood. Obviously, this is something to do once the weather moderates as you might run the risk of chilling the brood.

The advantage this method has over the Demaree manipulations is that you do not have to find your queen and contain her in the lower box. If there is a downside to this method, it would have to be the potential to chill brood because there are not enough bees to cover the brood. This method works well once the weather is settled. It also give the queen a lot more room to lay eggs as you have now "opened" up the brood nest. Open brood nests were very popular in the 1950s and 1960s.

If there was a downside to the "open brood nest" concept, not just checkerboarding, you end up with the potential of the queen laying eggs in the honey supers. You've basically given the queen a free reign of the entire hive, and by spreading out the brood frames, it seems to give her license to lay eggs anywhere she pleases. However, as the summer progresses, more and more nectar is stored higher up in the hive and the queen begins to lay more eggs in the lower boxes.

Often, the pupating bees in the upper boxes mature and move out of those cells in the upper boxes before the honey harvest, but you have basically given the queen wide-spread permission to lay eggs anywhere. This means I need to check my supers frame by frame to insure I'm not bringing home brood to the honey house (and times, I've even brought home a queen on those brood frames).

Further, if you are trying to shake bees or remove bees from honey supers, removing bees from brood frames is next to impossible. We'll talk more about this in a later chapter on harvesting your ton of honey.

I like to practice this open brood nest, but once the nectar flow starts, I will frequently go in and find my queen, then move her to the bottom box (or bottom two brood boxes), place a queen excluder over these boxes, then stack the other boxes (which may contain brood) and my honey supers.

What I'll get is a nice brood chamber below and an open area above dedicated to nectar storage.

Swarm Control:

Okay, you did your best to prevent swarming. What should you do when they want to swarm despite your best efforts and intentions? My first inclination is to give the bees the books I've been reading on how to prevent swarming. Obviously, they haven't been reading the same books as me!

But what do you do if you've done everything previously mentioned and you open your hive to find a dozen swarm cells? (Swarm cells are really pupating queen cells and most often—but not always--they are lined up on the lower edge of the frame).

If the bees still want to swarm, you need to shift from swarm prevention to swarm control.

How can you check to see if your swarm prevention is working? One thing I've heard older beekeepers suggest is to look on the bottom of the frames. This is where most swarm cells are located. If you want to run through a bee yard to see if they are preparing to swarm (or not), the easiest and fastest method is to crack open the hive and peer on the underside of the top brood box. If they are thinking of swarming, you'll see the swarm cells lining the bottom bars of the frames. And don't be surprised if you find ten to twenty swarm cells.

This is quick and dirty, but not foolproof by any measure. If you see capped swarm cells, you almost bet that your old queen has left with half of the bees. But this is not foolproof either. This is why I strongly recommend marking your queens.

If nothing is done, the first and oldest peanut-shaped queen cell will hatch. Now you have a virgin queen running around your hive. She may take a day or so to mature, then she'll take off with half the population. Now bear in mind, your old queen has left with half of the population. That was the "prime" swarm. Now the first queen cell hatches and this virgin queen leaves with half of the half that remained.

If they raised multiple cells, you'll have multiple "after" swarms, each succeeding swarm smaller than the swarm that preceded it. And it's possible your hive will swarm itself into extinction, or be so weakened they get robbed out or find themselves unable to store up enough honey for the coming winter.

If you see capped swarm cells, it's very possible your old queen has already left with half of the original work force. Now your job is no longer swarm prevention. You need to control the swarming impulse.

The older beekeepers like to go through and cut out or squish those queen cells every ten days. If the old queen has left (which is probably a given if the swarm cells are capped), then it's not likely you're going to need to do this in another ten days. There is no queen left to lay eggs, but if there are still young larvae present, one more round of squishing those swarm cells will be required.

How do you know if the old queen has left? Did you mark your queen? Marked queens are easier to find, particularly in a highly populated hive. The mark on a queen tells you her age and identifies her as a mated queen. If you should find a queen running around the hive, and she bears no mark because you were either too lazy or timid to mark your queens, you may have your old queen or you may have a virgin getting ready to leave with an after swarm.

The only way to insure your old queen is still present is to open the hive and check each frame. The only way to know if that queen you found is the old queen is to look at the paint that you applied to her thorax.

At this point, if I were to open a hive filled with swarm cells and I found my old queen with her marking, I have two choices. One choice is to squish all the swarm cells and close up the hive. Now I need to hope I found them all! But something is wrong and this hive has decided it's going to swarm.

By squishing all the swarm cells, I just delayed their intent. A hive that has decided to swarm is very stubborn. Tear out those swarm cells and they'll just rebuild them (provided they have age-appropriate larvae to make queen cells from).

So I can go through and squish swarm cells and plan to do it again in another ten days or I can pull out the queen and put her in a nuc box along with two or three frames of bees and brood. I will likely squish all but one swarm cell and allow it to hatch. As it is the only swarm cell, this queen will not leave the hive. She'll stay and go on her mating flight, then settle down to lay eggs.

By removing the old queen with only a few frames of bees, you create an artificial swarming experience. You don't lose half of your work force and you'll still likely harvest a nice crop of honey.

But all of the last five paragraphs have assumed you found your old, marked queen. So what if you can't find her?

If you are sure the old queen has left, cut out all but one swarm cell. This one remaining cell will emerge and take charge of heading up the colony. Your colony is already diminished and the likelihood of a honey crop flew out the entrance with the old queen. If your hive is really populated, leaving one queen cell may retain the potential for a honey crop, but it won't be the same as if you prevented the swarming impulse.

As you cut out all but one swarm cell, be careful, if you miss but one extra queen cell hidden along the side of a frame, the colony will still issue an after swarm. The presence of queen cells means there is something lacking in your management. Cutting them out is substituting emergency surgery for solid prevention techniques.

Alternatively, if you have a colony that has multiple frames with queen cells, you can divide up and split the colony into nuc boxes, giving each nuc a frame with one queen cell on it (squishing all the other cells). Then divide up the remaining frames of brood and bees, and to be most effective, move these nucs to a new bee yard at least two miles away. This will prevent the bees from leaving the nuc box and flying back to the original site.

The beauty of splitting up the colony is the nucs you create. Your honey crop is gone, but when the bees raise swarm cells, those resulting queens are usually quite productive as they were created during a time when nectar and pollen were abundant.

When you shift to swarm control, you've basically lost your honey crop, but at least you can come out of the season with several nucs headed by young queens. All is not lost. But I cannot stress enough, that once you find queen cells, you've lost your primary objective. So simply switch tactics and shift you focus.

Another method to avoid swarming is to pick a breed of honeybee that is less prone to swarm. Carniolans are supposedly notorious in their likelihood to swarm, because, it is thought, they have such an incredibly rapid spring build up of worker bees. They build up fast that the congestion causes them to swarm. Several beekeepers have lamented that they looked in on their Carniolans hives and things looked good. Then a week later, the swarms are pouring out of these hives.

That's the nature of swarming. Things look good, but the bees know what's really going on. And you need to remember that the impulse to swarm happens weeks before you see the swarm cells. If only the bees would communicate better. I'd just appreciate it if they would read the same books I'm reading.

Italians are less prone to swarm, or so I'm told. I have not found through my experience that any one breed of bee is more or less prone to swarm, but then I never really test them with the conditions that prompt swarming. I do everything I can to reduce swarming! The key is to prevent swarming, and if your prevention fails, you have to control swarming.

I also collect my fair share of feral swarms. A lot of beekeepers think I'm crazy in that I collect bees that have swarmed and the conclusion is that these "swarmy" bees are going to swarm on me, or at least be more likely to swarm than my domesticated counter parts.

I have not found this to be true. All honeybees have it wired into their DNA that swarming is a natural instinct.

Swarm Management:

I also find great joy in catching feral swarms. I take and receive swarm calls all over the county, but I also want to insure these are not from my hives!

If you can't prevent a swarm from happening, and it seems some bees will swarm no matter how much room you give them, I advocate using swarm traps or "bait boxes."

I greatly advocate hanging several swarm traps around your bee yard to catch those swarms before they get away. If you can't keep them from swarming, you can at least keep the swarm that gets out and catch it before it heads for parts unknown. One thing you can do is catch that swarm, hive it, then recombine it with a weak hive after eliminating the weaker queen.

More information can be found in one of my other books, *"Keeping Honey Bees and Swarm Trapping"* which can be found at www.createspace.com/4106626

Concluding Thoughts:

Maximum honey yields are obtained from a huge workforce of foraging bees, but to garner a huge work force you have to prevent swarming. Swarming will diminish and disrupt the economy of the hive and decrease the chances of achieving your maximum potential.

Work to encourage the queen to lay more eggs, give her ample room, foster a rapid spring build up, but work to prevent the congestion that incites a swarm. Give the foragers ample space above the brood nest to store incoming nectar. Expand the brood nest to give the queen ample room to lay eggs.

Sound management anticipates the conditions that leads to congestion and takes care of them to alleviate the swarming impulse.

This is the third factor in managing your hives for maximum honey production. Once you have stalled or redirected their energies, it's time to focus on supering.

Supering is the management of providing ample room so you can store tons of incoming nectar that the bees will ripen into tons of honey. That's the fourth factor.

Chapter 7: Super Intelligently

The Fourth Factor

The fourth factor in achieving maximum honey yields is to super intelligently. By supering intelligently I refer to a) protecting drawn comb; b) supering generously with drawn comb; c) add supers by "bottom supering; d) supering strategically with foundation if you don't have drawn comb; e) harvesting selectively when honey is ready; and f) rethinking the need for queen excluders.

Protecting Drawn Comb:

In order to produce lots of honey, the bees need to bring in lots of nectar. Since nectar is so dilute, you need to provide the bees with lots of room to store lots of this thin nectar.

In the ideal situation, you need to generously provide lots of drawn comb for lots of nectar that the bees will eventually cure into that proverbial ton of honey. Lots of drawn comb. Lots and lots of drawn comb. Don't hold them up by giving them foundation they have to draw out into comb. Give them drawn comb and the nectar will flow into it before your very eyes.

In a nutshell, the more comb you provide, the more nectar they can store. The more nectar they can store, the more honey they can make. The relationship is simple. If a medium super will hold about thirty-five pounds of honey and you only give them one super for the entire honey gathering season, then there is no way you're going to get more than thirty-five pounds of honey from that respective hive.

Your lack of super space limits the maximum amount of honey you can potentially harvest. Further, by limiting the super space, the bees will start to store the nectar in the brood nest and you run the risk of congestion that will trigger swarming.

I can't stress this enough: Give the bees plenty of room to store the nectar, and if you protect your drawn comb while in winter storage (which prevents you forcing them to draw out new foundation) you have no delay in providing the space to store and cure this nectar.

This drawn comb I refer to is the comb from last year that has been stored and protected from wax moths and mice. I can't tell you how aggravating it is to open a stack of unprotected supers only to have that messy film of moth webbing hold everything together.

If the frames have only been used for honey storage by the bees, I have less of a worry for moth damage than if the queen accidentally got up into the super and laid some eggs—but this is no guarantee the wax moths will ignore honey supers.

If you have old brood comb from a hive that died out, you have a moth-magnet. It needs to be protected. To be on the safe side, most beekeepers will protect their stacks of supers whether the comb has been used for brood or solely for honey production. Moths will still attack honey supers.

By the way, did you know there are two kinds of beekeepers? Yes, that's right. There are those who protect their honey supers from wax moths and those who wished they had!

Let's talk first about protecting comb, then let's move to the ideals and strategies of providing lots of room for nectar storage.

Drawn comb is your most valuable asset. When I was a small producer, I liked to freeze my combs if there was any indication that the queen had used these frames for brood rearing. Brood cells will be darker than the normal honey cells, and most of the darker portion will be in the middle of the frame. Since I gave my queens free reign of the hive and practiced an open brood nest, it was not uncommon to be harvesting honey from frames that once housed developing larvae.

Now let me also add, parenthetically, that some beekeepers will absolutely abhor the idea of the queen laying eggs into the comb that you'll use for honey production. There's just no way they'll let that happen. As I practice an open brood nest, it becomes a certainty that some of your honey supers will have been used for brood. In my operation, this is not the end of the world. To others, it's the most heinous crime in beekeeping.

But this isn't the first opinion that has been debated in the history of beekeeping. Sometimes we just have to agree to disagree. But I digress.

So to be on the safe side, I will go to great lengths to protect my drawn comb. Now back in those days when I was a small producer, I didn't care for the smell of moth crystals. It probably goes back to the days of my youth when our wool blankets were stored in a cedar chest with ample servings of moth balls. Every winter, when those wool blankets were brought out of storage, we fell asleep in those cold Minnesota winters with our brains stoked high on moth ball fumes.

To this day, I still don't like the smell of moth crystals (which are not the same as moth balls, though they smell basically the same). So back in my days as a small producer, I preferred to freeze my supers, then store them in the basement.

Freezing a few supers at a time in my chest freezer is no problem (well, no big problem until my wife found out). Brood cells with old larval casings are particularly attractive to wax moths and freezing for 24 hours will kill any hidden wax moth larvae and also the eggs.

When I froze my supers for 24 hours, I stored these supers in my basement. My basement is finished and free of moths and mice. But after I expanded and my operation grew, I no longer had room for every super in my basement and trekking up and down the steps quickly became impractical.

And my wife was home too often for me to sneak all those supers into the freezer.

I had dreams of finding a large, walk-in freezer like the commercial bakeries and butcher shops used, but none were available. And in reality, even if one were available, it wouldn't be cost effective to freeze all my supers.

Freezing supers is labor intensive, but really effective, and safe. Now I use an outdoor shed for the bulk of my supers. Supposedly a well-lighted shed reduces moth infestations, but if the moths want your frames and they are unprotected, they'll find them. Some guys will store their supers in a stack, but they alternate the supers by 90 degrees so light gets into the offset portion (and supposedly keeps the wax moths out).

This method, however, did not work for me. The wax moths, like some of my bees, did not read the same books on how to protect comb from being damaged.

I could still freeze my supers, but since there are times I have lots of supers and freezing is not practical, I will place everything into storage with the wax moth crystals. And remember, moth crystals are not the same as moth balls (but in reality, if you're reading this book you probably already know this).

If you shop some of the discount, "dollar" stores, you'll find sources of cheap moth balls which are the right chemical, para-dichlorobenzene, or PDB for short, and they're always available from the beekeeping supply catalogs often sold under the brand name of "Para Moth."

I only store "dry" comb without the honey residue. The wet combs from the extractor are given back to the bees to clean up before I store them. Then, after a winter in storage with moth crystals, the frames will need a couple of sunny spring days to "air out" before you add them to the hive for this year's honey crop. I use moth crystals sparingly, and by the time I'm ready to super for honey, the crystals have evaporated and a few days out in the sunshine prepares the supers for honey storage.

If the frames smell too much like moth crystals, the bees will ignore them. If I can get by without moth crystals, I would. But a super full of moth-damaged frames is totally disgusting. Not only is it disgusting, you destroy all the bees' hard work.

Wax moth crystals also deter mice from making nests in the stored boxes.

As an alternative, I've been using a different treatment with excellent results. There are other products on the market sold under the broad name of "Bt," or Bacillus thuringiensis. It is the subspecies of aizawai that works on wax moths. It's a powder you mix in water, then spray on your dry combs. I use a dedicated garden sprayer mixing three teaspoons per gallon. I apply the liquid as a fine mist to each side of the frame, then air dry before moving into my storage shed. It works really well and there's no smell.

It is certified as an organic treatment. For details, write a guy named, "Sundance," aka, Bruce Nyquist, 5777 77th Ave NE, Devils Lake, ND 58301. You can also find him on www.beesource.com

This same product was sold in most garden centers under brand names such as "Dipel" and "Certan." I should also note that this product is not specifically labeled for protecting combs from wax moths. It is, however, organic and safe for humans and bees, and it works.

At this point, protect your comb over the winter months. Protect your comb because you're going to need it the next year in the following spring for maximum honey yields. You want as many frames of drawn comb as possible if you want lots of honey. Too many beekeepers actually limit their bees' ability to make honey by denying them room to store nectar. Sometimes this denial is inadvertent and sometimes it's just a case of plain ignorance.

And some of my beekeeping buddies actually balk at buying extra supers. And yet just one year of honey will pay for that new super and all the frames and foundation needed to supply that super. If you take nothing else away from this chapter let it be this: give your bees lots of room, lots and lots of room and if possible, lots of frames of drawn comb.

The first step is protecting that drawn comb. Store it and protect it from wax moths and mice.

Super Generously with Drawn Comb:

To achieve high yields of honey, give your bees plenty of super space. Ideally, super generously with drawn comb.

Why do I encourage lots of supers and why do I stress drawn comb and not foundation? As the bees bring in the nectar, they need an incredible amount of immediate comb space to store this dilute substance. The greater the population of field bees, the greater the amount of nectar brought in, the greater number of frames of drawn comb required.

As the nectar comes in, it will come in faster than the bees can draw out new foundation to store the nectar. Or if your bees are like my initial foray into beekeeping with nucs and plastic foundation, they'll balk at drawing out the foundation and there will be no place to store the nectar.

If you don't have the room, or if the bees need to draw out foundation, or if they balk at drawing out new foundation, more nectar will be stored in the brood chamber. The congestive presence of excessive nectar in the brood area will encourage the bees to swarm.

Also, empty comb inspires and motivates the bees to get to work and fill it. Too few supers frustrates their work ethic, plus, if you don't provide enough super space, they'll begin storing honey in the brood chamber, which in turn crowds the queen and you'll trigger the impulse to swarm. I can't seem to reinforce this statement enough!

I hope by now you've committed that statement to memory!

Generally speaking, the impulse to swarm is reduced during the nectar flow, but if the queen is out of room to lay eggs because the brood chamber is clogged with nectar, they'll swarm. And swarming often takes place just before the main honey flow begins so it's a good practice to super early, and generously!

Also, if the bees have to draw out new foundation, they'll eat that incoming nectar as an energy source to produce the wax. It is estimated that it takes eight pounds of honey to produce one pound of wax. If you have to put on new foundation every year because you left it unprotected, your bees will not be leaving much honey for you.

Not only does it require the bees to expend more energy, I can guarantee you that if you spend a couple of weekends cleaning out moth-damaged frames and inserting new foundation (translation: $$$$), you'll do a better job of protecting your dawn comb. I should know. I've been there; done that!

I had an older beekeeper near me who only kept one hive. The hive was comprised of one 9-5/8" brood box and one 6-5/8" super. That's all. In the business we call this configuration, "a story and a half."

Every spring, about the first part of May, his hive would swarm. He didn't really care if they swarmed, but because he was a nice man who liked me, he'd call me to come out and catch that swarm. He was very generous in letting me have that swarm, and oddly, he didn't really care if his hive swarmed or not. He didn't want more hives, nor did he want more equipment.

Somewhere in the summer, he would pull out two or three of the frames from the top super. Because the hive was limited on space, the queen often used these supers for the brood nest. He would take a couple of frames into the kitchen and cut out the comb, then place the comb in a large bowl. His wife would mash the comb and lay it in a colander lined with cheese cloth. They let it sit for a couple of days. The strained honey was put in a couple of canning jars and they had all the honey they wanted.

He put the frames back into the hive and the bees filled the empty space with new comb.

Efficient? Not at all.

Did he super generously? Nope.

Did he care that they swarmed? Apparently not.

Did he manage his hive for maximum production? Not even close.

Did he fulfill his purpose and objectives for keeping bees? Certainly!

I tell that story because this old beekeeper was keeping bees the way he wanted, according to his wants and needs. But there is so much more potential, and the easiest way to accomplish that potential is to super generously. Give your bees all the room they need to bring in copious amounts of nectar. And if you can give them drawn comb, they'll fill it a whole faster than if they had to draw out that comb.

Bottom Supering:

My first basic point is to protect your drawn comb to make life easier on the bees (and you!).

My second basic point is to super generously. If you don't give your bees ample room to store nectar, they won't have room to make their maximum potential of honey. Give them room by giving them plenty of supers of drawn comb, and insure it is on the hive prior to the nectar flow.

My third basic point is this: "bottom supering" will provide opportunity for bees to move upward more readily than "top supering." You can provide all the room in the world, but if the bees won't move up into the super, then your honey yields will be diminished.

It sounds simple enough, but my first years of beekeeping did not turn out as well as I would have liked. I knew what I needed to do. First, I added plenty of supers of drawn comb. Second, I placed them on the hive before the honey flow started. Then I waited for the bees to fill them up, cap the honey so I could extract them.

And as I expanded, I had some remote yards 20 miles away. So when I went down to those yards, I wanted to put all the supers on all at once and not have to return until the capped supers needed to be extracted.

But here's where things started to break down. When I stacked three supers on these hives, the bees would either fill up two of them (ignoring the top super) or they would "chimney" and store nectar into the middle six frames of all three supers (ignoring the outer two frames on each side).

Then I started supering more intelligently. When the nectar flow started, I placed one super on top. The bees were naturally drawn into this super to store nectar. When it was about 60 to 70 percent full (that is six or seven of the frames full of nectar), I added a second super. But I placed this second super UNDER the existing super.

This is called "Bottom Supering." Yes, it's a whole lot easier and less time-consuming to simply put that new super on top of the existing super. But if you want your bees to get up into that super, it's more effective to place the new super under the existing super. This is particularly true of you are trying to get the bees to draw out new foundation.

Also, as you pull off that existing super, check the two outer frames on each side. Chances are real good they bees have not filled these out, or if they have, chances are real good they have ignored that side of the outer frame that faces the wood.

So what I'll do, before I bottom super, is to pull out the outer two frames on each side of this existing super (four total), then slide three of the inner frames to the right side and three more frames to the left. Then I place the four frames that used to be on the outside to the inside of this super.

This manipulation will encourage the bees to use the full set of frames in your super. And I might also add, that as I expanded, I purchased an electric, vibrating uncapping knife. The knife works better if I only place nine frames in my supers, as most commercial beekeepers do. The capped comb sits a little higher than if you used the complete set of ten frames.

So I relocate the outer frames to the inside of the super, then pull that super off. I set a new super on top of the brood area then set the old super on top of it. That's bottom supering and it works wonders at pulling the bees up into that new super.

As the flow commences, I do it again. The 60-70 percent rule is not set in stone. Generally, once the bees start moving nectar up into the existing boxes, bottom supering will help in getting them to move into a new super. Then as you need to add more supers, add them under the existing supers and on top of the brood chamber.

Supering Strategically With Foundation:

And up to this point, all I've emphasized is drawn comb. If you have drawn comb, please, please, please take care of it. And if you got it, for Pete's sake, don't leave it in your honey house when the nectar starts flowing and the plants start blooming in the springtime. Get those supers on your hives!

If you don't have drawn comb, your strategy will be different if you are introducing plain foundation. Instead of putting nectar into drawn combs, your bees will also invest more energy and resources into drawing out the foundation rather than putting that energy into the production of honey.

Statistics vary but it is estimated that eight pounds of honey are required for one pound of wax production. (And it's interesting that no one know where this figure came from. We've recited it enough that we've come to believe it). If for no other reason, protect your drawn comb.

If you have drawn comb, wonderful. Use it. But if you don't, it's not the end of the world. In order to best draw out foundation, especially if you still want high yields of honey, start with only one super, and again, start early. You may need to "crowd" the bees just a little bit to force them to move up into the super, so do not necessarily think about adding another brood box at this point. Force the bees to move up into the super.

When you add this first super, and if it's plain foundation, DO NOT use a queen excluder to keep the queen out of your super. In fact, if a few eggs were laid in a super it would hasten the process of getting that super drawn out. For a host of reasons, bees are reluctant to move up into a super of plain foundation.

But once they do, it's an easy process to keep them moving upward. And if the queen has laid a few eggs, they'll come up without much fuss. They seem to move up if you don't give them too much physical room in the brood area. But watch your hives so they don't get the urge to swarm.

When I'm introducing new foundation, I start my supering process with only one super of foundation, and I don't get overly concerned if the queen decides to lay a few eggs in it. Obviously, the pupae will be all hatched by the time you come to harvest the honey so it's no big deal.

While it's still early in the spring, I begin with that first super, I may continue to feed my hives a little syrup with feeders on the top using my special feeder screen. This continues to draw the bees upward and they work on drawing out the comb in preparation for the nectar.

And as I'm moving more and more supers to nine frames of drawn comb in my supers, I highly recommend you place ten frames in that super if the frames are plain foundation. Nine frames of foundation will give the bees way too much space between the frames, and unless the honey flow is really intense, you'll get comb drawn out between the frames. This seems to be especially true if you use the plastic foundation. Then their work is wasted as you try and sort out the mess. Nine frames of drawn comb is fine, but stick with ten frames if you are using foundation until it's fully drawn out.

Second, as you use foundation, you might want to start with one super and consider feeding a little syrup to get them started. Put the super on well before the honey flow and feed your syrup. Use a nectar-like syrup of 1:1, unless you want to dilute it further to 1 part sugar to 2 parts water.

It is the opinion of other beekeepers that the weaker syrup is consumed in the production of wax and the "heavier" syrups are stored in the cells for honey. You want wax production; you don't want to "mess up" your beautiful honey with stored sugar syrup.

Either way, the syrup will give the bees the energy to draw out the comb. This is also a neat trick if you are starting out in your first year and you don't have much aspiration about having any honey to harvest. What syrup is stored, along with incoming nectar, will eventually be consumed by the bees.

Feeding syrup early will also fool the bees into believing the nectar flow is on. I find feeding helpful for that first super of foundation in mid to late April when the weather around southeast Missouri is unsettled. It is not uncommon to have an entire week of cold, damp windy weather.

In the absence of syrup, or in the absence of a nectar flow, the bees will generally ignore foundation and it won't be drawn out into comb at all. A little light sugar syrup keeps them interested in drawing out that foundation.

In order to maximize your nectar flow, the foundation has to be drawn out ahead of the nectar flow. In place of comb, the bees have to draw out the foundation one super at a time. And don't be afraid to open up that first super after the bees have had a chance to get things started. Pull out the outer frames, create a vacant space in the middle of the super and put those outer frames back into the middle of those ten frames.

If the brood chamber is bursting with brood, I'll put on another brood box on top of the reversed boxes just to give the queen more room. By all means, checkerboard those frames if the weather is settled. Then I keep an eye on the rate at which they fill the top super. When another super is necessary, bottom super.

And as I've said before, the trick to stay ahead of the bees' needs. Anticipate their requirements and offer the resources they'll need. Stay ahead of the curve.

Selectively Harvest If Honey is Ready:

If I'm using drawn comb, I will keep an eye on the top super and remove individual frames of capped honey to be extracted. Usually the middle frames get capped first. I take out those capped frames then add another frame of drawn comb to replace it. Then I take that capped frame home and extract it (more on this in the next chapter).

I believe the bees know how much honey is up in that super, and if honey is removed, they'll work harder to bring in more nectar. If I don't have a frame of drawn comb, a frame of foundation will do. Take out the honey when it's ready and give them another frame of drawn comb. They'll wonder where the honey went to, but they'll quickly decide they can't quit working yet and they'll keep filling empty frames as long as the nectar is flowing.

Some years when the honey flow has been intense, I've been short of supers with drawn comb. As the bees fill and cap full supers of ripened honey, I would hurry up and extract that full super, then added the empty supers back to the hive later that same day. You don't have to harvest all your honey in one day.

I like to take my honey when it's ready and return the wet frames to be refilled. This way you keep reusing your frames and you don't need as many for these maximum yields of honey you hope for. The bees will keep on working as long as there's empty comb to fill.

More on this in the next chapter.

Rethinking the Queen Excluder:

If you are starting out with a super of plain foundation, do not put on a queen excluder. Bees will not go up through a queen excluder and draw out foundation. It's as simple as that. Do not use a queen excluder at this point if you're trying to draw out foundation.

If you really feel the need to use a queen excluder, put it on after the bees have drawn out at least one full super. Then when you bottom super with a new super of foundation, you can place the queen excluder under that new super to keep the queen down. The existing super of drawn comb and ripening nectar will pull the bees up through the excluder.

Again, do not add the queen excluder if you are using foundation in that initial super. I made this mistake then complained in my ignorance how the queen excluder was nothing but a "honey excluder." The drawn comb will draw the bees to the top and a queen excluder is a hindrance to getting bees to draw out that first super of foundation.

With the addition of the second super, you've passed the biggest obstacle to using foundation. The bees will feel comfortable coming up into the supers and with the honey flow coming on, they'll draw out the foundation in the new super rapidly. Keep adding supers, but only as the last super you added has been drawn out into comb. Add supers from the bottom, placing the new super of foundation above the brood box but still under the other supers of drawn comb.

Again, you may want to reverse the brood boxes when you add the new super of foundation, but with the honey flow on, the situations that trigger a swarm are greatly diminished. Bees do not want to leave their hard work. If anything, reversing the brood boxes just keeps the queen down below and out of the honey supers. However, do not be alarmed if the queen has moved up into the honey supers. Catch her and move her down into the brood box.

It should be noted that lots of beekeepers do not use queen excluders. They manage their bees to keep the queen down low and the incoming nectar up high. If you do use a queen excluder, I would highly recommend the use of an upper entrance. You can buy shims to create that entrance in the stack of supers or you can drill a 1" hole in your supers. Drill the hole about halfway between the handhold and the bottom edge, but never in the handhold itself.

And then there are the majority of beekeepers who believe I should be shot for drilling a hole in my supers. But again, it's another difference of opinion.

One of the nice things about honeybees is that they will store nectar and honey toward the top of the hive. If the queen does move into the supers, it is very likely those cells of larvae and pupae will mature before the super needs to be harvested.

As those frames and supers are filled with incoming nectar, the queen will continue to move downward in the hive. You may not really need an excluder at all. However, you will have dark comb in your honey supers.

You'll also want to provide an upper opening for ventilation. Don't simply crack open a space between two supers or you'll incite a riot of robbing. I use a screened inner cover, then I lift the telescoping cover with a stick or scrap of wood to allow the moisture from the evaporation process to escape.

When the honey flow is slowing down, you'll need to begin consolidating the supers of nectar by removing the capped honey. Sort through the supers and place all the capped honey aside to be taken to your honey house. Some beekeepers like to wait until the season is all done, then take off entire supers of capped honey.

I like to take the frames of capped honey off, one at a time if the super is not entirely full, and place them into one super and take those to my honey house to extract. Then I consolidate the other partially filled frames and let the bees finish them off. There is no point in harvesting honey that is not capped.

If you aren't ready to extract those frames of capped honey, then consolidate the capped honey into one or two supers and put those supers on the top of the hive, then place the frames of uncapped honey underneath them.

One of the things you are attempting to do at this point is push the bees down into those lower supers to finish off ripening the nectar. You may want to add a super of plain foundation under the supers needing ripening.

As the honey flow is about over, and as I've taken all of my capped frames to be extracted, I'll stack the supers of unripened nectar and uncapped honey with my wet supers out in the middle of the yard to be robbed out and any left over nectar to be carried back to the hives. They'll store it in the bottom brood boxes (because the supers are removed) and I'm ready to shift to my mite control measures. I'm also ready to move those supers into storage after providing my protection from wax moths.

At this point I'm down to two brood boxes on most of my hives. The major work of the beekeeper's season has come to an end, or at least the intensity is lessened. From this point, I allow the bees to forage for what is available without worrying about harvesting this honey (and things really begin to slow down so they need this honey for the winter). I may need to consider feeding weaker hives or new swarms that I catch.   I then turn my attention to hives that I will split into fall nucs and a summer queen production for my fall requeening project.

Use a queen excluder, but only with drawn comb, and only after the bees have put in some nectar.   The presence of nectar will get the bees moving through the excluder and up into the super. And don't be in too much of a rush to add that excluder. Early on, before the honey flow comes on with a vengeance, put a super on the hive. Allow the bees to add some nectar, but don't bother with the excluder at this point. It will come later.

Anytime during the honey flow that the queen moves up into the honey supers and lays eggs is the time to add the excluder. Simply catch her, put her below, put on the excluder and allow time to release the larvae before extracting. The presence of eggs and larvae will attract the worker bees to the comb which will help get the nectar evaporated. Then, as the pupae hatch, the bees will use that cell to store nectar.

Once you get nectar into a super, the bees are more likely to continue putting nectar in the super. Getting the initial deposit is what is difficult, and using an excluder with bare foundation will make it impossible to get the process started.

The fourth factor to maximize your honey yield is to have lots of drawn comb, but it also requires intelligent supering. The key is to give generous supers of drawn comb, but if you don't have comb, only add supers of foundation as the bees need them. If you limit the space for nectar, you limit the yields of honey.

As you add supers, I like to "bottom super." This is especially important if you have plain foundation, and less important but still helpful if you have drawn comb. It also means rethinking the use of queen excluders.

Chapter 7: Harvest Expediently

(Harvest Early; Harvest Often)

The Fifth Factor

How does one go about harvesting their honey? Most beekeepers I know wait until the crop is all done blooming. For some beekeepers (like us in Southeast Missouri), this happens in the middle of July when the weather turns really hot, really dry and everything turns to dust.

For others (like those south of us), this happens when a frost kills everything back. The time when the major nectar-producing crops finish their blooms varies from region to region.

However, the consensus from most average beekeepers is to wait until the nectar has ceased coming in, then it's the time to start making harvest plans.

When these beekeepers open their hives, they want all of the frames in each super to be 100% capped. Then they get their honey house (or the garage or kitchen) cleaned, prepped and ready. They line up some part-time help (usually the in-laws). Then they wait until the weekend (as most of us still have full-time jobs), and then hope the weather cooperates.

These guys go out and "pull" all their honey, all at the same time. The word, "pull" is used to describe the means by which the honey super is "pulled" off the hive, brought home to extract. They mostly will use some foul-smelling liquid to drive the bees out of the super, down into the brood raising area in the brood boxes.

Most of these guys will have used a queen excluder to keep the queen in the lower boxes so all the frames in the upper boxes are pure, harvestable honey. Then they'll go out and pull all the supers that sit above the queen excluder once the bees have been driven below.

At this juncture, there are many ways to clear the supers of bees. My point is that most, average beekeepers do it this way. But I didn't sign up to be average!

So all these supers come home, all at once. The honey is extracted in one big, long, exhaustive extracting party (often because extra help is home for the weekend). It makes for a long weekend. And the weather has to be cooperative.

The empty supers, still wet with a little honey, are set out in the back yard to be cleaned (robbed out), then set into storage with wax moth crystals (P.D.B.). Then the emphasis in the bee yard is moved to mite control and winter preparations.

A New Way to Do It!

Let me offer a different way that will greatly increase the amount of honey you can harvest. But let me warn you, it will also take more work. For me, it's a great trade-off with more work equaling more honey. And further, you don't have to harvest your honey in one big, exhaustive marathon (providing the weather works in your favor).

The nectar flow in my region ends around the 4th of July. A little more nectar will trickle in the first half of July, but for the most part, my honey producing season is over. I could go out and pull all my supers and call it a season.

Or I could wait until Labor Day and run the risk of the bees eating up my honey crop.

However, I've had capped honey on half of my frames back in the early part of June. That's about a month ahead of the scheduled end. And what are the bees going to do with it? They're going to keep it until winter unless I go out and pull it off.

And if I don't pull it off, I run the risk of the bees telling each other, "There! We are set for the winter. Everybody take the day off we've got our whole hive full of winter stores."

So my ideal is to take the capped honey off as soon as it is ready, extract it and return those wet frames to the hive. Empty comb inspires the foragers to keep working.

To harvest my honey early and often, I start in early to mid June. I go out to a bee yard in the late afternoon and open hives, pulling out just the frames of capped honey. Most of these frames are in the middle of the super, and it's mostly the top super that has the capped honey. The number of frames will vary from colony to colony and yard to yard. A lot of the honey production is weather dependent.

I bring a wheel barrow or garden cart with me, and in it, several supers of drawn comb or new foundation. I will go through my hives and pull out the two or three frames of capped honey from each hive. Given a bee yard of twenty hives, that amounts to four to six total supers of honey. I replace these frames of capped honey with new, empty frames from my wheel barrow.

Some of my yards will have entire supers filled. If so, I'll take them now. If I have a lot of capped honey, and if I have to add a whole super of empty comb, I'll make sure I bottom super the newer supers. But if it's just two or three frames, they'll be in the top super. And at this time, I'll also find a lot of frames of uncapped honey—too early to harvest, just yet.

I might do the same to another two yards in the same general area. I like to pull the frame and gently brush the bees off, or as alternative, give the frame a smart shake. I don't need the stinky stuff that drives the bees downward. I have used it with good results…until I came home and wanted to come in the house. My wife threatened to burn the clothes I was using. That stinky stuff permeates everything.

So I brush or shake my bees off the few capped frames I'm pulling.

Once placed in my wheel barrow, these frames need to be covered as I collect them or I'll begin to incite robbing. But the good news is I'm not in the bee yard for very long. Further, if the honey flow is going on, robbing is not such a problem than if the area is experiencing nectar dearth. The bees don't have a lot of time to find my supers of capped honey in the wheel barrow.

I stack the supers in my pickup truck, then I head for home. If I have more yards in the immediate area, depending on what I've pulled from this yard, I may stop at another yard.

Now I've got my honey house set up to extract honey for the whole season. So I immediately unload my truck setting the hive bodies and supers in the honey house to prevent robbing. I wish I had a "hot room" where I could keep the supers warm (even reducing the moisture content of the honey a point or two), but I don't.

When I get home from two or three yards and get the truck unloaded, it's generally dinner time. So I eat, then about seven o'clock I go outside to the honey house and start extracting. I've got a bench where I uncap my frames, then I have a rectangular tub where I set twenty uncapped frames. This tub was custom built to the same dimensions of the hive body so the frames hang and drip until I'm ready to load them in the extractor.

In this tub, they'll continue to drip, and this tub drains into a five-gallon bucket. When I have twenty frames uncapped, I stop uncapping and load those twenty frames into my twenty-frame extractor.

Thankfully, my motorized extractor will run while I uncap twenty more frames, moving the uncapped frames to my tub. When the extractor is finished, I unload the twenty frames into the empty supers, load twenty more uncapped frames from my tub and turn on the extractor. It spins slowly and easily while I uncap twenty more frames and place them in the drip tub.

The extractor empties into five-gallon buckets and I set that bucket of honey on a stand to be strained. The whole design of honey houses is another topic for another day (seems we have this same idea of needing "another day" popping up now and then).

Needless to say, I have a small, one-man operation when I bring ten to fifteen supers home. The extraction process is like a pipeline where I bring supers of capped honey into the honey house. The honey goes into five-gallon buckets and the supers go out the door to the back yard to be robbed out. I usually finish up and clean up around ten or eleven o'clock that night. It makes for a nice, relaxed evening.

The next day, weather permitting, I'll go out to another couple of yards. Site location and my choice of bee yards are often linked to regular routes I can run in an afternoon. They may be five miles apart, but I try and link several bee yards in the same general direction away from my house.

So I'll go out and pull another four to six supers from a couple of yards late in the afternoon, then bring the supers back and extract them after dinner. By the second day, my cappings from the previous day have drained sufficiently to be moved. My previous day's supers are robbed out to be reused and reinserted into another hive the following day.

Once I get going, it's easy to take the previous day's supers, now robbed out, with me to the next bee yard to replace the frames of capped honey I'm taking home. This reduces my need for too much additional equipment.

My honey harvest system is like a corrupt political system: Rather than "voting early and often," I harvest early and often.

What's the benefit to this method? For starters, once that frame of honey is capped, the bees have no immediate use for it. A capped frame is finished for the season. I also believe that the bees sense how much honey they need and if given enough spare room, will continue to bring in nectar.

But if their space is filling up with honey and the honey is capped and ready for winter, I sense the bees begin to back off. They know there is no more room for more nectar. They know their need for honey is taken care of for the coming winter.

But what if that honey is removed? It's been my experience that the bees will sense an urgency to gather more nectar and store more honey if their supply is running low. So in my devious trickery, I'll take the honey and induce them to store more.

By harvesting early and often, you offer the bees more opportunities to continue to fill supers with nectar. By harvesting each day instead of one big extracting party at the end of the season, you spread out your work and your labor.

It's not nearly so exhausting and if the weather is inclement today, I can wait until tomorrow. Or if a family obligation comes up, I don't need to worry about this giant extracting expedition hanging over my head.

Having worked with, and for, large beekeepers who bring in supers by the truck load, I can tell you there is nothing more tedious than those long sessions of nothing but extracting super after super. It gets to be a long day, most of which you spend on your feet. And the scenery doesn't change until the last super is done.

Another Benefit:

There is another benefit to harvesting smaller batches from selected bee yards that most people fail to capitalize on: varietal honeys.

As I harvest my honey in smaller batches from selected fields, I notice that some honey will have specific characteristics, characteristics different than another field five miles away. Some honey is lighter, some honey is darker. Some honey is flavored by certain crops, even when I have no idea where those bees are foraging.

I keep honey from certain fields separated and segregated from the honey harvested from other fields. What I sell at my farmer's market stand is honey that is known by the variety of the plants or location. It is known in the industry as "varietal" honey.

A varietal honey is a honey that is identified by its variety of flower or location. It means my honey will vary from one location to another, and even my early harvested honey from my honey harvested later that summer.

I have hives in the north (Cape Girardeau County) that is ready about a month earlier than the extended nectar flow to my south (Benton County). Swampy areas have different flowers than upland farm fields. You create a market niche by keeping your honey separate, and to keep it separate, you need to harvest in smaller batches.

I also have samples of my varietal honeys, as well as ice cream tasting spoons, at my farmer's market stands so people can sample the difference. If you Google "ice cream tasting spoons" you'll find several resources for these disposable spoons. They cost about a penny each.

When you harvest your honey in one big spasm, you cannot keep it separate. You cannot keep it segregated, but this might not be that important to you. Maybe working the big weekend when your help is off from their college classes is ideal.

Another Benefit:

Another benefit to harvesting early and often is diminishing the threat of the small hive beetle. I have, sadly, on several occasions, brought home a load of supers, but I had meetings later that night. So I tell myself, "Tomorrow, first thing, I'll extract that honey."

One benefit to extracting right away on the same day is that the supers are still warm with all the residual heat from the afternoon sun and the heat generated from within the hive. They uncap real easy and the extractor slings out the honey with little effort. It just makes for a great night of extracting.

When you leave the supers sit for a day, they cool down. When you get busy, or you can't harvest them right away because you're "tired" or someone needs a ride or you forgot your child's band concert, one day soon turns into another day. After three days, you run the risk of small hive beetle eggs hatching in your supers.

Small hive beetles are rather innocuous as adult beetles. The beetles run around the hive. They eat bee eggs and fresh larvae, as well as pollen. But when the hive is stressed (like when you open the hive and stir around in those supers), the small hive beetles lay eggs in the supers. Hundreds and hundreds of eggs. The eggs hatch into larvae, and it's the burrowing larvae that prove to be the most destructive.

When the bees are present, they generally take care of the small hive beetles. But once you remove the supers from the bees, the remaining beetles lay eggs and the eggs hatch into the most destructive, burrowing larvae. They burrow through the honey and it begins to ferment. The best remedy is to harvest your supers and extract them as soon as possible.

I like to drain my cappings for twenty-four hours, then set them out in the yard for the bees to clean up and rob any residual honey. I bought large, flat plastic "totes" for this purpose. After a day or two of robbing, I melt the cappings down into blocks of wax. If I leave them for any length of time, the small hive beetles will be laying eggs in those cappings and you have another mess on your hands.

My treatment of the old cappings if fairly simple. After they are robbed out, I pile the cappings into one of those old fashioned roasting pans (famously present at most church pot-luck dinners). You can buy them at any one of a hundred department and discount stores, priced anywhere from $29 to $49.

If you shop at garage sales, you can pick up a used one for less than $5. They have a pan that works like a double boiler and the heating element does not come into contact with the pan.

I pile in my cappings, add about a quart of water, then set the roaster pan on a low simmer. By the next day, the cappings are melted and I can skim out the floating debris with a screened-wire strainer.

After I clean out the floating pieces, I let the pan cool until the next day. There will be a layer of debris on the bottom of the cooled wax block, and a bunch of junk that settled into that quart of water on the bottom. I kick out that block of wax to use later. For the most part, it's safe to store the wax as it is.

The Final Push:

There will come a time, however, when the last nectar has come in and it's time to pull all the supers. Again, for my region, this is about the middle of July. It will be earlier if the rainfall is short. About three weeks before this time, sometime in the middle to late June, I'll reorganize my hives.

To reduce the swarming impulse and to open up the brood nest giving the queen more room to lay eggs, I do not use a queen excluder during the honey flow. This means I've got a good chance that I have brood in my honey supers. This is no big deal to me, but to some people, it's a HUGE crime.

About the third week in June, I'll go back through my hives and pull more frames of capped honey and give them empty frames. I'll also dig through the supers and find the queen. It will be easier to find her if you've taken the time to mark her.

But we've already had this discussion, haven't we?

How to effectively find the queen is also another great topic for another day! Even when you mark her, she's elusive at times.

At this point I'll catch her in a queen catcher (sold by every major supply catalog), tear down the hive by removing the supers, then I'll top the lower two brood boxes with a queen excluder and release her into these lower boxes.

At this point, the use of queen excluder is to limit the queen to the lower brood boxes with ample time for any brood above the excluder to mature and hatch out.

Over the next three weeks, any egg she laid in the upper boxes will hatch, pupate and emerge. That's when I come through and pull all those supers. My nectar flow is pretty much done and it's time to consolidate the hive. If I remove the queen by the third week in June, install an excluder, my supers will be free of all brood by July 15th. That's when I can make my final push and pull off all the honey.

By moving the queen down under an excluder, the bees in this highly populated area in the supers will backfill the emerging brood cells with nectar and convert it into honey. Most, but not all of these frames will be capped honey. The lower portion under the queen excluder is open to the queen to lay more eggs.

What About Uncapped Frames?

A question I'm faced with is what to do with uncapped frames when I bring in all those supers. Basically, you have two choices. You can put them right back on the hive and let the bees eat up that nectar or you can set them out in the back yard and allow them to be robbed out. That nectar will now be stored in the lower boxes as winter stores.

My choice is to let the bees rob out any unripened nectar and leave the super empty. From here, these supers go into storage, protected from wax moths.

By no means should you try and extract open frames of ripening nectar, particularly if nothing is capped on that side. Now if part of the frame is capped, it's a different story. You might be able to extract it depending on how ripened the nectar is.

There are some beekeepers who use the "shake" test to see if they can extract this partially capped frame. They take a frame of uncapped nectar and with the open side facing the ground, they give it a shake. If nectar falls out in drips, then it is too wet to extract. If it does not drip out, it is mature enough to extract.

I've done this with good results, but if there is nothing sealed, I'll leave it. I've also pushed my luck with open cells if one side of the frame is totally sealed and the other side is mostly sealed. Generally, if I can cover the open cells with my palm (fingers together) it will extract without any problems.

My big idea for my northern hives is to pull all those supers off, extract the capped honey, let the bees clean out the uncapped honey, then move those supers to storage. Now I can start my mite treatments without worrying about messing up my honey. Now I can feed my medicated or treated sugar syrup during the nectar dearth during August. This is an ideal time for bees to cure syrup for winter stores.

Having often procrastinated, I've gotten myself into a jam and tried to feed during the blustery weather in October. I would rather do it in August, and the bees will thank me for my efforts.

Also, with my honey all harvested (ideally) by the first of August, I now switch gears. I start looking forward and thinking about next year. I start making and equalizing my nucs for the winter, and August 1st is not too early to be thinking about next year!

A Last Word:

A last word on supers: Protect them! Protect your drawn comb as if it is gold.

You will get better yields if you insert frames of drawn comb into your supers than if the bees have to draw out foundation. This is particularly important to keep the bees happy and productive. They will fill up drawn comb a whole lot faster than having to draw out foundation. And additionally, it takes more honey to draw out the additional comb.

But we've talked about that already, haven't we?

If you're looking to harvest a monster crop of honey, super intelligently and harvest expediently.

And this brings us to the conclusion of the five factors that are within our control. But there are still a couple of variables to work in order to harvest this monster crop of honey. That's the next chapter.

Chapter 8: Land Management

Location, Location, Location

An Optional Sixth Factor

There is a sixth factor, but not one that is particularly practical to most beekeepers. It's like the frosting on the cake, and unless you have a great cake, no amount of icing is going to work.

This sixth factor is found in three parts that have a bearing on your ability to bring in an abundant honey crop. These three parts are: 1) plant honey plants, 2) move your bees to better forage, and 3) spread your bees out to different "out yards."

And then, let's also remember the rather unpredictable nature of the weather. All the plans in the world will go out the window when the weather works against you. I've seen extreme cold and heat, drenching rains and droughts so bad nothing would grow. The weather is always something to contend with. Still, we do our best to work with it.

Plant Honey Plants:

First, consider establishing a land-based production system of honey plants in which you sow large fields to produce the blooms which produce ample amounts of nectar. Most people don't have large tracts of land, and those that have the land want something with a greater return than that which honey provides.

If you have a small acreage, consider sowing several acres to a variety of clovers, and a selection of other plants suitable for your area, sown to provide a blooming season spread out over the summer, to provide a variety of nectar and pollen. Sometimes nature provides the best forage and sometimes you have to plant it. Consult your local extension office for the best forage crops, most of which will be legumes and clovers. Plant a variety that will give your bees an extended window of blooms.

Give consideration to road ditches and grassy areas that are not suitable for other crops. Our family farm in Minnesota used to have several "water ways." These were the places where rain water would run and erode bare land. My family left them in grass to catch the run-off and reduce erosion.

Then we rented out the land and the tenant promptly plowed them under because he didn't like the fields to look like patchwork quilts. My father acquired a new tenant and the state conservation district paid to have them seeded back to grasses and legumes. This land is rendered "useless" by modern agricultural standards, but is a great resource for honey plants.

If you have vacant corners or ravines, steep hillsides, plant these areas to clovers and other nectar producing plants. There will be grassy areas around groves and pastures which can be sown to honey producing plants.

You can sow the ditches along the road ways, but you'll have to make sure the county won't spray for weeds. When I kept bees in Minnesota, the county would not spray if I came into town and picked up the colored markers. The county sprayed to kill the broad leaf plants, of which, clover is susceptible. They would not spray, if requested, but I also had to agree to keep the noxious weeds under control.

Currently, I have quite a few hives on farms that back up to Interstate 55. The massive roadway has broad banks and medians of clovers and blooming weeds. Every so often, someone asks me if I mind all that "automobile pollution" in my honey. Quite frankly, I don't think it's really that much of a problem. Pollution is everywhere. But I have free access to hundreds of acres of blooming clover for much of the summer.

I also have my bees on farms with CRP ground and cattle pastures. If you have an agreeable landlord, you can move your bees to farms instead of trying to acquire your own land base. CRP ground, or for that matter, any of the current government "set-aside" acreage, cannot be cut or grazed so the honey plants are free to bloom.

The disadvantage of using your own acreage for land-based systems of honey plants is what to do with the plants after they bloom. By the time the blooms fade, the plants are no longer nutritionally viable for a good hay crop. Still, someone may want to cut the stems for roughage. Grazing isn't an option because the plants are too old and the livestock pretty much ignore them. Clover could be plowed under as a green-manure crop, but still, you tie up too much land for a conventional agricultural enterprise.

If you know someone with a large tract of land, particularly if this land is not utilized for modern agriculture, or is not suitable to row crops, ask them if you can sow some seed for your honeybees. This plan, of course, means you have to have your bees near this land. And most land is in use. There are some tracts of land tied up in a variety of government programs which pay farmers not to farm (CRP).

If you can find someone who has open stretches of cover crops, ask him or her if you can put your bees out on his ground. Be sure and check with the local officials. Bees are not considered a problem, but some of this government "set aside" ground has to be sprayed or mowed to control noxious weeds. Ask to see if you can sow some clovers or other blooming plants. Winter is the ideal time to "overseed" deadened patches of grass.

Some farmers like to plant "wildlife plots" with blooming plants that they will later use to hunt upland game in the fall. These can also make nice plots for honeybees. In our area, several varieties of annuals work for turkey and sunflowers are popular for doves.

I sow the ditches and roadsides near my bee yard by broadcasting seed. Across the road from one of my yards is a gravel pit with lots of "wasted" space. I asked to sow the sides of this property with a variety of clovers. The owner didn't mind when I suggested the clover be sown to keep topsoil from washing into his pits where he was removing gravel.

Some of my bees are close to pastures which give some blooms before the cows eat the plants. I've got some nearby farms that have "set aside" acres. The government has different plans to reduce the crops sown on fragile land.

Most of this ground is sown to grasses and the government sometimes tells the farmer when they can mow, when they have to mow, and some of this ground must be disced or burned to control weeds.

If honeybees can't find the naturally occurring floral sources for maximum honey production, provide the flowers for them. Plant some honey plants. You can do everything else to maximize your honey production, but if there are no flowers, there will be no honey. Take advantage of open areas and plant them to honey producing plants.

Move Your Bees:

Second, if you can't plant crops, move your bees where the crops are grown. This is the basis for migratory beekeepers. It is my hope to find permanent places for bees rather than moving them, but some regions run out of flowers and other locations come into bloom. If you want to get the maximum honey from your colonies, consider moving your bees to where the plants are blooming.

South of me are regions of soybean and cotton farms which provide great amounts of honey. If you can't plant crops to provide nectar, move the bees to the crops. It takes a lot more work to move bees, but if you want to maximize your honey production, you need to have blooming crops nearby.

I don't move but a fraction of my bees, mostly because of the inconvenience and time involved. If I was serious about becoming a migratory beekeeper, I'd have my hives on pallets and move them with a forklift.

An alternative to a forklift is to have your hives secured to a trailer. I've seen trailers with hives strapped down. The trailer is moved to the new location, the straps are released and supers are added. After the honey harvest, or when the trailer needs to be moved, the straps are replaced and tightened down, the trailer is hooked up to a pick-up truck and the whole operation is effortlessly moved to the next location.

This arrangement works better with pollination contracts, and often pollination contracts don't necessarily lend themselves to maximizing honey production.

Sometimes the work of moving the bees isn't justified if you have a challenge marketing your honey. It is easier just to leave them in one place and get what you can from the available crops, then leave enough honey to carry them through the bloomless period and on into winter.

Spread Out Your Bees:

Third, consider spreading out your bees. If you have too many hives concentrated in one area, the bees will begin to compete for the blooms. This is especially true if you have a lack of good nectar sources in your area. If it is possible, try locating your bees at different locations.

How many bees fit into one out yard? I don't really know. It depends on how many, and what kind of plants are in the area that provide nectar. Obviously, wide open pastures of grass will do you no good. Solid forested areas are not real dependable for supplying nectar for honey production. If you live near areas that are sprayed heavily for weeds or insect pests, then you also have a problem.

As in real estate, the best advice for gathering large amounts of nectar may be location, location, location. If you don't have a good location, move your bees. And if you do have a good location, don't overload the out yard with too many hives.

And again, what constitutes "too many" is a much discussed question. And if you don't have many blooms, consider planting some crops. If you don't have the opportunity to plant crops, spread your bees out so they don't compete.

The Weather Wild Card:

And let's not forget that reality that you need cooperative weather. This is a variable you cannot control and it is simply a factor you'll have to take into consideration. You can plant all the clover in the world, or move your bees to the perfect pasturage, but if the weather won't cooperate, you just won't get an abundant honey crop.

But remember what this manuscript is about. It is about maximizing the potential your bees have to bring in the most nectar and make the most honey. I've noticed in years with uncooperative weather patterns, there are things you can do to get the most honey from your hives, given the circumstances that exist, but my yields have been disappointing.

In comparison from year to year, the yields may be less, but when I talk to my regular beekeeping buddies who only do what they have time to do or feel like doing, my honey yields surpass their hives. Everything is relative. To work to maximize your honey yields can make a good year a fantastic year, and a really poor year into one that is manageable, perhaps even survivable.

Maximizing potential is really a two-pronged approach. Be proactive and do the things that will gain the most advantage, but also work to minimize those things which are limitations. And sometimes, when you work to take advantage of the best options available to you, you also inadvertently take care of the limitations that would normally hold you back.

And never discount the weather. Some years it works for you and some years it will do everything to set you back. Do what you can do and take the weather as it comes. Diversify your locations so the weather won't affect all your hives. Given the fact that all things are equal, sound and attentive management will bring in higher yields of honey and minimize the variables beyond your control. And weather is perhaps the greatest variable beyond our control.

Chapter 9: A Final Thoughts

My goal is to manage my hives to gain the maximum amount of honey that is possible, given all the funky variables and fickle circumstances that plague my life. And I work hard at it and I believe the return on my investment is very satisfying. I invest a lot of time, energy and passion into my bees. They reward my hard work and proactive planning. I love keeping bees.

But I continue to run into that age-old problem of having enough time to do all the things I want to do. I found that as I added more hives, it took more time. That's a no-brainer.

As I expanded my hives, I had more honey to market. But as my bee operation was taking more time, I had less time to market my honey. My marketing efforts began to compete with my hive management, and those began to conflict with my family obligations and work commitments.

I will continue to fight this battle, though I continue to work smarter, not necessarily harder. I've hired some help, which is a hard thing for me to do. No one seems to want to work as hard as I do, nor do they see beekeeping with the same passion as I. I've been trying to delegate a lot of issues, but in all things, my standards are awfully high.

Still, I cling to my goals and my purpose in keeping honeybees. My goal is to maximize my skills and manage my hives for their fullest production potential.

I firmly believe that the success of any endeavor is a clear vision of your purpose. Once you know what you definitely want, the battle to attain that vision is half won. Whatever you decide to do, know why you're doing it, then pursue it with passion.

My last little bit of parting advice is this: Do everything that is within your power, and trust the things that aren't will work themselves out. Give the bees every advantage possible and don't let your laziness or procrastination become their stumbling block.

Accept this world for what it is, not that you like everything that happens, but recognizing the interrelatedness between our management and their productivity.

Then do everything within your power to take advantage of life's opportunities.

Afterword

Okay, we had a forward/foreword, now we have an afterword (the *word* that comes *after*).

Here are a couple of things to remember when you go about keeping bees. First, it matters little what books you've read, the bees will have their own way of doing things. They seldom read the same books you've been reading anyway. However, they will tell you if you're doing something right or something wrong. If they prosper, you're doing well! If the hive crashes and dies, then you need to rethink what you're doing.

Second, there is no substitute for experience. It's a lot like learning to swim. You can read all about it, you can do all the exercises on dry land, you can watch a hundred videos, but until you get into the water, you won't know how to swim.

And the best swimming lessons I've had is when I got in over my head. You learn very quickly to sink or swim. I chose to swim. Beekeeping is like that. Once you get your bees, you'll start learning. You'll have to.

Third, nothing important merely happens. That's my father-in-law's advice. The important things take planning and preparation. They seldom just happen on their own. So go out and start making some plans.

Lastly, take my advice and feel free to revise it. Find your own way. We all have to row our own boats and hoe our own gardens. There are many ways to keep bees. I described how I did mine and what worked for me. Feel free to experiment, revise, revamp, rethink and totally retool my approaches for what works for you.

Mostly, make it fun. If beekeeping is too much work, I highly recommend stamp collecting. But whatever you decide to do, don't do it half-way. You get out what you put in.

Appendix: The Making of a Beekeeper

So you're looking for "coaching" on what makes one "successful" in beekeeping. Some people ask me if I think they have what it takes to be a successful beekeeper.

First of all, success is relative and individually defined. At the most basic level, if you can keep bees, keep them alive, enjoy how you keep them, I'd say you're successful.

Second, don't let anyone disrespect you for only having a couple of hives, and don't apologize by saying, "Well, I only have a couple of hives."

If you keep bees, you're a beekeeper. And I believe just about anyone from any walk of life can learn to become a beekeeper. However, I have found ten characteristics that tell me whether or not a person will be successful at keeping bees.

I'll stay away from specific techniques and particular equipment usage, but there are several key characteristics of successful beekeepers that transcend location and style of management, even size of the operation. Here they are, my coaching points for beekeepers who want to be successful:

1) Passion - this is the energy that is derived from having a vision of what you want, and what you want to do with this endeavor we call beekeeping. It is the mental picture you hold in your head and heart as the ideal. Everything else funnels into this vision.

2) Purpose - you can't have unbridled passion or you'll end up running in all directions. Purpose is the reason why you are keeping honeybees. It controls and directs your passion. Purpose brings chaos into order.

3) Planning - the key to planning is to have the end in mind. Where do you want to go? Where do you want to grow? Where do you want this hobby/business of

beekeeping to take you? We develop goals as steps to that ultimate end.

4) Preparation - Some people call me the luckiest beekeeper, but luck is nothing more than preparation meeting opportunity. Successful people are prepared for the opportunities, large and small, that come our way each day. Purpose helps us to recognize them; passion excites us to act upon them.

5) Patience - There is no such thing as an overnight success. Patience does not despise small beginnings. Patience preserves.

6) Persistence - My father-in-law was famous for saying, "Nothing important merely happens." Success takes work, and persistent beekeepers plan their work and work their plan.

7) Participate - Get out there and try something new. Don't be afraid to take a few calculated risks. Push yourself to keep learning. Innovate. Think outside the box.

8) Pardon - learn from your mistakes and move on. There's no value to continue to beat yourself up over things you did wrong. Turn failure into a learning experience on how things are not done.

9) Pliable - Blessed are the flexible for they never get bent out of shape. Sometimes you have to backtrack and change plans. Sometimes circumstances humble you into finding a different way to do things. Successful people must be pliable.

10) Pause and Perceive- take frequent opportunities to step back and assess your goals and vision. Is it working for you? Take notice of your environment, become aware of changes that leave you working today's problems with yesterday's solutions.

And the beauty of these 10 points is they work for just about any profession or hobby.

About the author:

Grant F.C. Gillard began keeping honeybees in 1981 following his graduation from Iowa State University from the College of Agriculture. He started out with twenty hives on the family farm in southern Minnesota and now resides in Jackson, Missouri where he tends around 200 hives...for now.

He sells honey at several local farmer's markets as well as raising his own locally adapted queen honeybees. He is a husband of twenty-six years and father to three grown children.

He pastors the First Presbyterian Church in Jackson, Missouri, as his "day job." He frequently threatens to retire to devote his full energy to beekeeping, but secretly, he enjoys the ministry and is greatly appreciated by his congregation.

After serving for the past nineteen years in this position, he has become more of a community chaplain and is often simply called, "The Bee Guy," or "The Honey Dude," depending upon which generation recognizes him at Wal-Mart.

He is eternally grateful to members of his congregation who have graciously allowed him to dabble in this hobby, and for his restraint of not turning every sermon into an illustration on beekeeping. He is a past-president of the Missouri State Beekeepers Association.

He is a frequent conference speaker and may be contacted at: gillard5@charter.net Contact him regarding his availability for your next event.

Other books of interest may be found at:

www.CreateSpace.com

and

http://www.Smashwords.com

Or visit Grant's personal web site where you can look at his other publications and read sample chapters:

www.grantgillard.weebly.com

(click on the "My Books" tab at the top)

Grant also blogs under revgrant1 at:

www.expertscolumn.com

and

www.xomba.com

You can find him on Pinterest and Facebook, or just jump on any search engine and "Google" him.

Made in the USA
Lexington, KY
01 April 2015